The Opportunity Analysis Canvas

Sixth Edition

Dr. James V. Green

Publication Data
Green, James V.
The Opportunity Analysis Canvas / James V. Green
Sixth edition
1. Entrepreneur. 2. Innovation.

ISBN: 979-8392014989

For Jamesia, Alexandra, and Vivian.

Thank you for giving me the opportunity to be a husband and dad.

Access Code for the Online Evaluations

For students enrolled in a course that has adopted the online evaluations
for The Opportunity Analysis Canvas, please contact your faculty
for instructions on how to register with your unique access code.

ABOUT THE AUTHOR

An award-winning educator and entrepreneur, Dr. James V. Green leads the education activities of the Maryland Technology Enterprise Institute (Mtech) at the University of Maryland. As its Managing Director of Learning and Development, he leads the undergraduate and graduate courses and programs in entrepreneurship, innovation, and technology commercialization. He has created and led a host of innovative programs and activities that serve over 1,000,000 entrepreneurs and innovators from over 175 countries. With more than twenty publications to his credit, he is a thought leader in educating entrepreneurs and innovators worldwide.

In 2020, he was recognized with the Dean's Outstanding Performance Award in Teaching for Professional Track Faculty. This award recognizes one professional track faculty annually for excellent contributions in teaching. He earned first prize in the 3E Learning Innovative Entrepreneurship Education Competition presented by the United States Association for Small Business and Entrepreneurship (USASBE).

Prior to joining the University of Maryland, Dr. Green held founder, executive, and operational roles with multiple startups, including WaveCrest Laboratories (an innovator in next-generation electric and hybrid-electric propulsion and drive systems, acquired by Magna International, NYSE: MGA), Cyveillance (a software startup and world leader in cyber intelligence and intelligence-led security, acquired by QinetiQ, LSE: QQ.L), and NetMentors.Org (the first national online career development eMentoring community).

Dr. Green earned a Doctor of Management and an MS in Technology Management from the University of Maryland Global Campus, an MBA from the University of Michigan, and a BS in Industrial Engineering from the Georgia Institute of Technology.

CONTENTS

1. Overview

There is nothing more powerful than an idea whose time has come.

Victor Hugo

Poet, novelist, and dramatist

THE ORIGINS OF THE OPPORTUNITY ANALYSIS CANVAS

The Opportunity Analysis Canvas is based on my experiences of teaching over one million students at the University of Maryland, Coursera, and edX, and mentoring hundreds of startups. This canvas began over 10 years ago with my doctoral dissertation titled "Educating entrepreneurship students about opportunity discovery: A psychosocial development model for enhanced decision-making." While this dissertation title may sound complicated, the basic idea is that before drafting business models and writing business plans, aspiring entrepreneurs need to see and think about problems and solutions differently than others.

As I explored this topic of entrepreneurial opportunity analysis, I recognized a pattern that could be identified. With that identification and understanding, I saw that it is a process that could be taught.

Before beginning this book, I tested various ideas and approaches of teaching over many years at the University of Maryland. These activities engaged thousands of my students on campus in readings, assignments, projects, and mentoring that led to dramatic improvement in their entrepreneurial opportunity identification and analysis skills.

The outcome of this opportunity analysis journey, and the proven success of its teaching, is this book. It is my hope that by understanding the principles and patterns of The Opportunity Analysis Canvas you will become more effective in identifying and analyzing entrepreneurial opportunities while realizing your personal and professional goals.

The Opportunity Analysis Canvas is a tool for identifying and analyzing entrepreneurial ideas. Structured as a nine-step experience, the canvas is segmented into: thinking entrepreneurially with an entrepreneurial mindset, entrepreneurial motivation, and entrepreneurial behavior; seeing entrepreneurially with industry condition, industry status, macroeconomic change, and competition; and acting entrepreneurially with value innovation and opportunity identification.

The Opportunity Analysis Canvas

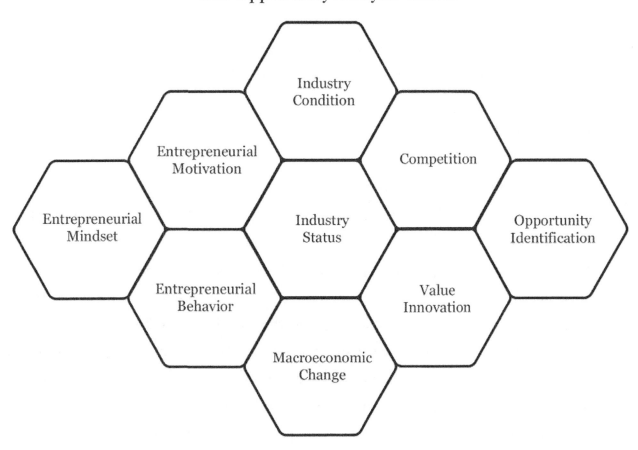

Without the idea for the product or service, neither business model nor customer discovery can begin. It is this first step of defining the idea that The Opportunity Analysis Canvas aims to fulfill.

How Can You Best Use This Book?

This book's structure directly aligns with the Opportunity Analysis Canvas, as each of the nine steps is addressed in a dedicated chapter. The focus of each chapter is to first introduce you to the topic. This provides a background on the subject and describes its relationship to entrepreneurship. Tools including research databases and reference materials are highlighted. Tips and techniques for how to develop your skills and knowledge are then presented. Then, a featured entrepreneur is profiled. Lastly, challenge questions are posed for you to develop your opportunity analysis abilities.

These nine steps are explored in three parts:

- **Steps 1 – 3: Thinking Entrepreneurially.** Thinking in this context is influenced by individual mindsets, motivations, and behaviors. The first part of the book addresses these first three steps of the Opportunity Analysis Canvas.
- **Steps 4 – 7: Seeing Entrepreneurially.** The second part of the book examines seeing entrepreneurially, which requires that you have a "big picture" perspective. This means that you recognize and understand the economic forces impacting your ideas as well as industry and competitive factors that exist now and in the future. With dedicated chapters on industry condition, industry status, macroeconomic change, and competition, each of these steps is explored in detail.
- **Steps 8 – 9: Acting Entrepreneurially.** As you develop your abilities to think and see entrepreneurially, you are better prepared to act in part 3 of the book. With attention to value innovation and opportunity identification, you can transform your entrepreneurial ideas into action.

2. Introduction

Don't start a company unless it's an obsession and something you love.

If you have an exit strategy, it's not an obsession.

Mark Cuban

American entrepreneur, investor, and

owner of the NBA's Dallas Mavericks

WHAT IS AN ENTREPRENEURIAL OPPORTUNITY?

An entrepreneurial opportunity can be defined as a chance or opening to create a new product or service or improve an existing one. It is a situation where an entrepreneur identifies a need or problem in the market that has not been adequately addressed and develops a product or service to meet that need. An entrepreneurial opportunity can also arise from a change in the market, such as the introduction of new technology, a change in consumer behavior, or a shift in the competitive landscape.

One of the key aspects of an entrepreneurial opportunity is that it has the potential to generate profits. To be an economically viable opportunity, a business idea must be financially sustainable, meaning it should be able to generate enough revenue to cover its costs and provide a reasonable return on investment.

Another important characteristic of an entrepreneurial opportunity is that it must be scalable. This means that the business should be able to grow and expand over time, either by increasing its customer base or by introducing new products or services.

An entrepreneurial opportunity can be a new business concept or an improvement on an existing idea. In either case, the entrepreneur needs to have a clear understanding of the market and the competition to be successful. This requires conducting research and analysis to identify the target market, its needs and preferences, and the strengths and weaknesses of potential competitors.

Entrepreneurs who can identify and capitalize on entrepreneurial opportunities have the potential to achieve significant success. However, it is important to note that not all entrepreneurial opportunities are equally attractive or feasible. It is important for entrepreneurs to carefully evaluate and assess each opportunity to determine whether it aligns with their skills, interests, and resources, as well as the market demand and competitive landscape.

In summary, an entrepreneurial opportunity can be defined as a chance or opening to create a new product or service or improve an existing one. It must be financially sustainable and scalable, and the entrepreneur must conduct thorough research and analysis to assess its potential for success.

HOW ENTREPRENEURIAL OPPORTUNITIES TYPICALLY ARISE

Entrepreneurial opportunities can arise in a variety of ways. Common sources of business opportunities include changes in technology, shifts in consumer behavior, emerging trends or demographics, and new regulations or policies.

One of the most common ways that entrepreneurial opportunities arise is through technological innovation. Advances in technology can create new opportunities for businesses to develop and market new products or services. For example, the rise of e-commerce and mobile technology created new opportunities for businesses to reach consumers and sell products through online channels.

Shifts in consumer behavior can also create new opportunities for entrepreneurs. For example, the growing interest in health and wellness has led to a surge in demand for products and services in this industry, from healthy food options to fitness programs and wellness retreats. Demographic shifts, such as the aging population, can also create opportunities for businesses to develop products and services to meet the needs of these new markets.

Entrepreneurial opportunities can also arise from emerging trends and cultural shifts. For example, the growing interest in sustainability has led to new opportunities for businesses to develop environmentally friendly products and services, and the rise of the sharing economy has created new opportunities for businesses to provide peer-to-peer services and experiences.

Finally, changes in regulations and policies can also create new opportunities for entrepreneurs. For example, the legalization of cannabis in many U.S. states has created a new industry with opportunities for businesses to provide products and services related to cannabis cultivation, distribution, and retail.

To identify and capitalize on entrepreneurial opportunities, entrepreneurs must stay informed about market trends, consumer behavior, and changes in regulations and policies. They must also conduct thorough research and analysis to identify unmet needs or gaps in the market and develop innovative solutions to meet those needs. By staying attuned to these various sources of business opportunities, entrepreneurs can position themselves for success in the dynamic and ever-changing business landscape of the United States.

ENTREPRENEURIAL VENTURES STARTED BY COLLEGE STUDENTS

Many successful technology-based businesses have been founded by college students. These businesses have leveraged innovative technology and disruptive business models to create new markets, transform existing industries, and generate significant value for their founders and investors. Here are some notable examples of successful technology businesses started by college students in recent years:

- **Dropbox:** Founded in 2007 by MIT students Drew Houston and Arash Ferdowsi, Dropbox is a cloud storage and file sharing service that allows users to store and access files from any device. The company has over 700 million registered users and is valued at over $8 billion.

- **Snapchat:** Founded in 2011 by Evan Spiegel, Bobby Murphy, and Reggie Brown at Stanford University, Snapchat is a social media platform that allows users to share photos and videos that disappear after a brief period. The company has grown to become one of the most popular social media platforms in the world, with over 280 million daily active users.

- **Stripe:** Founded in 2010 by brothers Patrick and John Collison of MIT and Harvard, respectively, Stripe is a payment processing platform that enables businesses to accept online payments. The company has grown rapidly, with a valuation of over $100 billion as it processes billions of dollars in transactions each year.

- **Warby Parker:** Founded in 2010 by four University of Pennsylvania students, Warby Parker is a direct-to-consumer eyewear company that sells prescription glasses and sunglasses. The company disrupted the traditional eyewear industry by offering affordable, stylish, high-quality glasses and has grown to become a billion-dollar business.

These examples highlight how college students have been able to identify and capitalize on technology-driven business opportunities in a variety of industries. These businesses have transformed the way we live, work, and communicate and have created significant value for their founders, investors, and customers.

WHY MANY COLLEGE STUDENTS DO NOT START COMPANIES

Despite the increasing popularity of entrepreneurship education and the success stories of several young entrepreneurs, many college students do not start companies for any of the following reasons:

- **Lack of Experience and Skills:** Starting a company requires a wide range of skills, from business planning to marketing to financial management. College students may not have had the opportunity to develop these skills or gain the necessary experience to succeed as entrepreneurs.

- **Fear of Failure:** Starting a company can be a risky proposition, and college students may be reluctant to take on this risk. Fear of failure can be a major obstacle for some students who worry about the financial and personal consequences of a failed venture.

- **Lack of Funding:** Starting a company often requires a significant investment of time and money. College students may not have the financial resources to launch a business or may be unable to secure funding from investors or lenders.

- **Focus on Academics:** College students may be focused on their academic studies and not have the time or energy to devote to starting a company. Balancing the demands of coursework and extracurricular activities can be challenging, and some students prioritize their academic performance over entrepreneurial pursuits.

- **Uncertainty About the Future:** Many college students are unsure about their career paths and may be reluctant to commit to starting a company before they have explored other options. The prospect of starting a company can be daunting for students who are unsure about their long-term goals or interests.

- **Lack of a Viable Business Idea:** Finally, some college students may simply not have a viable business idea or not know how to identify and evaluate potential opportunities. Without a strong business concept, it can be difficult to gain traction as an entrepreneur.

While these obstacles can be significant, there are a plethora of resources available to help college students overcome these challenges and launch successful businesses. Entrepreneurship programs, mentorship opportunities, and access to funding and resources can all help aspiring entrepreneurs get started and achieve their goals.

WHAT IS THE MINDSET REQUIRED FOR ENTREPRENEURS?

Entrepreneurship is not just a set of skills or a specific set of actions – it is a mindset. To be a successful entrepreneur, you must cultivate a particular way of thinking that enables you to identify opportunities, take risks, and persist in the face of obstacles. Here are some key elements of the mindset required for entrepreneurs:

- **Creativity:** Entrepreneurs need to be able to think creatively and come up with innovative ideas that can disrupt existing markets or create new ones. They need to be able to think outside the box and see things in new ways.
- **Risk-taking:** Starting a company requires taking significant risks, from investing time and money to facing potential failure. Entrepreneurs need to be comfortable with uncertainty and able to take calculated risks in pursuit of their goals.

- **Adaptability:** Markets, technologies, and consumer preferences are constantly evolving, and entrepreneurs need to be able to adapt quickly to changing circumstances. They must pivot their business models, change strategies, and respond to new challenges as they arise.

- **Persistence:** Starting a company can be a long and arduous process, and entrepreneurs must persist in the face of setbacks and failures. They need to be able to stay focused on their goals and continue working towards them, even when the going gets tough.

- **Vision:** Entrepreneurs must be able to see the big picture and envision a future that is different from the present. They need to be able to articulate a clear vision for their company and inspire others to join them on this journey.

- **Drive and Passion:** Finally, entrepreneurs must have a strong drive and passion for what they do. They need to be motivated by a sense of purpose and a desire to make a difference in the world. This drive can help them overcome obstacles and achieve their goals.

Cultivating this mindset can be challenging, but it is essential for success as an entrepreneur. By focusing on developing these qualities and characteristics, aspiring entrepreneurs can increase their chances of success and build globally impactful businesses.

WHAT IS ENTREPRENEURIAL OPPORTUNITY ANALYSIS?

Entrepreneurial opportunity analysis is a process that involves identifying, evaluating, and pursuing potential business opportunities. It is a critical step in starting a new business or launching a new product, as it helps entrepreneurs determine whether an opportunity is worth pursuing and how to best approach it. Here are some key elements of entrepreneurial opportunity analysis (EOA) and why it is important for aspiring entrepreneurs:

1. **Idea Generation:** The first step in entrepreneurial opportunity analysis is idea generation. This involves brainstorming potential business opportunities and identifying areas of unmet need or inefficiency in the marketplace.
2. **Screening and Evaluation:** Once potential opportunities are identified, they need to be screened and evaluated to determine their feasibility and potential for success. This involves conducting market research, analyzing the competitive landscape, and assessing the resources and capabilities required to pursue the opportunity.
3. **Business Planning:** If an opportunity is deemed feasible and viable, the next step is to develop a business plan. This involves outlining the strategy, operations, financial projections, and marketing plans for the new business.
4. **Implementation:** Once a business plan has been developed, the next step is to implement it. This involves putting the plan into action, securing funding, building a team, and launching the business or product.

ENTREPRENEURIAL OPPORTUNITY ANALYSIS IS IMPORTANT FOR ENTREPRENEURS

There are several reasons why entrepreneurial opportunity analysis is important for aspiring entrepreneurs, including:

- **Avoiding Pitfalls:** Entrepreneurial opportunity analysis helps entrepreneurs avoid common pitfalls and mistakes that often derail new businesses. By thoroughly researching the market, competition, and potential customers, entrepreneurs can identify potential risks and obstacles that may arise and develop strategies to overcome them.

- **Identifying Profitable Opportunities:** Entrepreneurial opportunity analysis helps entrepreneurs identify business opportunities that have a strong potential for profitability. By analyzing market trends, customer needs, and emerging technologies, entrepreneurs can identify gaps in the market and create products or services that are in high demand.

- **Developing a Solid Business Plan:** Entrepreneurial opportunity analysis helps entrepreneurs develop a solid business plan that outlines the key elements of the new venture. This includes the strategy, operations, financial projections, and marketing plans for the business. By having a clear roadmap for the business, entrepreneurs can secure funding, build a team, and launch the business successfully.

- **Maximizing Resources:** Entrepreneurial opportunity analysis helps entrepreneurs maximize their resources by identifying the most effective and efficient ways to pursue a business opportunity. This includes identifying the necessary resources and capabilities required, as well as the most effective ways to acquire these resources.

- **Minimizing Risks:** Entrepreneurial opportunity analysis helps entrepreneurs minimize risks by identifying potential challenges and developing strategies to mitigate, avoid, or overcome them..

In summary, entrepreneurial opportunity analysis is critical for aspiring entrepreneurs because it helps them avoid pitfalls, identify profitable opportunities, develop a solid business plan, maximize resources, and minimize risks. By conducting rigorous analysis and evaluation, entrepreneurs can ensure that their new ventures are based on sound ideas with a strong potential for success.

How Entrepreneurial Opportunity Analysis Differs from Business Plan Development

Entrepreneurial opportunity analysis (EOA) and business plan development are two critical steps in the process of starting a new business or launching a new product. Although these two steps are related, they serve different purposes and require different skills. Here is a comparison between EOA and business plan development:

- **Purpose:** EOA is a process of identifying, evaluating, and pursuing potential business opportunities. It focuses on understanding the market, competition, and customer needs while identifying the best ways to create value for customers. Business plan development, on the other hand, is a process of outlining the strategy, operations, financial projections, and marketing plans for the new business.
- **Scope:** EOA is a broad and exploratory process that involves researching and analyzing various business opportunities. It is an iterative process that involves multiple cycles of brainstorming, screening, and evaluation. Business plan development is a more focused and specific process that builds upon the results of EOA. It involves outlining the details of the new business.

- **Skills:** EOA requires skills in research, analysis, and creative thinking. It requires entrepreneurs to be able to identify unmet needs in the market, research market trends, and evaluate potential opportunities. Business plan development, on the other hand, requires skills in finance, marketing, and operations. It requires entrepreneurs to develop financial projections, identify marketing strategies, and design operational processes.
- **Timing:** EOA typically comes before business plan development. It is the first step in the process of starting a new business or launching a new product. It is a process of exploring. Business plan development, on the other hand, comes after EOA once a new business has been chosen.

In summary, entrepreneurial opportunity analysis and business plan development are two critical steps in the process of starting a new business or launching a new product. EOA is a process of identifying, evaluating, and pursuing potential business opportunities, while business plan development is a process of outlining the strategy, operations, financial projections, and marketing plans for the new business. While they serve different purposes and require different skills, both steps are essential for the success of any new venture.

Summary

In this chapter, we have introduced the concept of entrepreneurship and discussed the importance of entrepreneurial opportunity analysis for college students interested in starting a new company. We have explored the definition of a business opportunity, the reasons why many students in entrepreneurship classes do not start real companies, and the mindset required for entrepreneurs to succeed.

We have also examined examples of successful technology businesses started by college students in recent years, including companies such as Stripe, Dropbox, and Snapchat. These companies demonstrate that college students can successfully start and grow a business with the right mindset and approach. We have discussed the importance of taking action once you have an idea for a new product, as well as the benefits of EOA in helping aspiring entrepreneurs identify, evaluate, and pursue potential business opportunities. We have also compared EOA to business plan development, highlighting the differences in purpose, scope, skills, and timing between these two critical steps in the process of starting a new business.

In conclusion, entrepreneurship is a challenging but rewarding path for college students interested in starting their own business. EOA requires skills in research, analysis, and creative thinking, as well as a mindset of curiosity, flexibility, and persistence. By taking action and applying the principles of EOA, college students can increase their chances of success and turn their ideas into successful businesses. In the next chapter, we will dive deeper into the EOA process and provide practical tips and tools for aspiring entrepreneurs to identify and evaluate potential business opportunities.

3. The Evolution of Entrepreneurial Opportunities

The critical ingredient is getting off your butt and doing something. It's as simple as that. A lot of people have ideas, but there are few who decide to do something about them now. Not tomorrow. Not next week. But today.

Nolan Bushnell
Founder of Atari

Entrepreneurial opportunities are the lifeblood of the entrepreneurial process. Without them, entrepreneurship would not exist. In this chapter, we will delve into the foundational elements of entrepreneurship and discuss classical definitions of entrepreneurial opportunities from some of the most prominent thought leaders in the field. We will explore how modern interpretations of entrepreneurial opportunities differ from classical definitions and examine emerging opportunities for entrepreneurs.

Entrepreneurship is a multifaceted and dynamic field that has evolved significantly over the past few decades. Today, entrepreneurship is often associated with innovation, risk-taking, and the ability to create value in new and innovative ways. As such, identifying and pursuing entrepreneurial opportunities has become a critical component of the entrepreneurial process.

Classical definitions have provided a solid foundation for understanding what entrepreneurial opportunities are and how they should be approached. However, modern interpretations of entrepreneurial opportunities have evolved and expanded to include new areas and fields of innovation. This has led to a broader definition of what constitutes an entrepreneurial opportunity and opened up new possibilities for aspiring entrepreneurs.

In addition to exploring classical and modern definitions of entrepreneurial opportunities, we will also examine emerging opportunities for entrepreneurs. As technology and society continue to evolve, new and innovative areas of entrepreneurship are emerging. These areas provide exciting opportunities for entrepreneurs.

Finally, we will discuss how large companies approach entrepreneurial opportunity analysis and decision-making. While many of the tools and techniques used by large companies may be applicable to entrepreneurs, there are also key differences in how large companies and entrepreneurs take that approach. By understanding these differences, aspiring entrepreneurs can learn from the successes and failures of large companies and apply these lessons to their own entrepreneurial ventures.

Overall, this chapter will provide readers with a broad understanding of entrepreneurial opportunities and equip them with the tools they need to identify and pursue new and innovative business ideas.

THE IMPORTANCE OF IDENTIFYING ENTREPRENEURIAL OPPORTUNITIES

Identifying entrepreneurial opportunities is the starting point for any successful entrepreneurial venture. Without a viable opportunity, it is nearly impossible to create and sustain a successful business. The importance of this starting point lies in the fact that opportunities provide the foundation for the development of a new business. By identifying and pursuing entrepreneurial opportunities, entrepreneurs can create value for themselves and society.

One of the primary benefits of identifying entrepreneurial opportunities is exposing the potential for creating new and innovative products or services that could disrupt existing markets, create new ones, and generate significant profits. By identifying entrepreneurial opportunities, entrepreneurs can create value in ways that were previously unknown.

In addition to the potential for creating new and innovative products or services, identifying entrepreneurial opportunities is important because it allows entrepreneurs to create businesses that align with their passions and interests. When entrepreneurs pursue opportunities they are passionate about, they are more likely to be motivated, engaged, and committed to the success of their ventures.

Moreover, identifying entrepreneurial opportunities is essential for promoting social and economic development. By identifying opportunities to create value, entrepreneurs can create jobs, stimulate economic growth, and contribute to the betterment of society. Furthermore, entrepreneurial ventures often create a ripple effect that encourages innovation and entrepreneurship in others, which in turn drives further economic growth and development.

In conclusion, identifying entrepreneurial opportunities is critical for discovering successful and sustainable entrepreneurial ventures. It allows entrepreneurs to create new and innovative products or services, align their businesses with their passions and interests, and contribute to social and economic development. By understanding the importance of identifying entrepreneurial opportunities, aspiring entrepreneurs can take the first steps towards building successful and fulfilling careers.

FOUNDATIONAL ELEMENTS OF ENTREPRENEURSHIP

Entrepreneurship is the process of identifying, creating, and pursuing new opportunities to create value through the fabrication of new products, services, or businesses. Entrepreneurship involves taking risks, generating innovative ideas, and adapting to changing environments to establish and grow sustainable businesses that generate economic and social value.

Intrapreneurship is a form of entrepreneurship that takes place within an existing organization. Intrapreneurs are employees who work within a company but take on an entrepreneurial mindset to create new products or services, improve existing processes, or create new business units within the company. Intrapreneurship encourages creativity, innovation, and risk-taking within an organization and can help companies stay competitive by adapting to changing market trends.

Social entrepreneurship is using entrepreneurial principles to create and run a business that generates economic and social value. Social entrepreneurs use their businesses to address social problems and create positive social change. Social entrepreneurship is not solely focused on profit but rather on creating social and environmental value.

Startup entrepreneurship, on the other hand, refers to starting a new business from scratch. Startup entrepreneurs are individuals who identify new opportunities, devise a business plan, and secure funding to bring their ideas to life. They take on significant risks and are responsible for building the entire infrastructure of their businesses, from product development to marketing and sales.

Overall, entrepreneurship is a multifaceted concept encompassing a variety of approaches and strategies. Whether it is intrapreneurship, social entrepreneurship, or startup entrepreneurship, the core principles of entrepreneurship remain the same: identifying new opportunities, taking on risks, and creating sustainable businesses that generate value for both the entrepreneur and society.

THE IMPORTANCE OF INNOVATION AND RISK-TAKING

Innovation and risk-taking are essential components of entrepreneurship, whether it is in the context of a startup or an established corporation. Startups and corporate innovators who prioritize innovation and risk-taking are more likely to develop new products and services, improve operational efficiency, and stay ahead of their competitors.

For startup entrepreneurs, innovation and risk-taking are critical for success. The startup world is characterized by uncertainty, and the ability to identify and take advantage of new opportunities is what sets successful startups apart from those that fail. Entrepreneurs who are willing to take risks are more likely to try novel approaches, experiment with new business models, and create new products and services that have the potential to disrupt entire industries.

For corporate innovators, innovation and risk-taking are important for staying competitive in rapidly changing markets. Large companies that prioritize innovation are more likely to develop new products and services that meet the changing needs of their customers. In addition, corporate innovators that are willing to take risks and experiment with new business models can create new revenue streams and expand their market reach.

However, it is important to note that innovation and risk-taking can also be dicey for both startups and established companies. In the startup world, failure is a common occurrence, and entrepreneurs who take risks may end up losing their investment. For corporate innovators, taking risks can lead to short-term losses or negative public perception.

Ultimately, the key to successful innovation and risk-taking is to balance the potential rewards with the potential risks. Both startup entrepreneurs and corporate innovators need to carefully evaluate each opportunity and determine whether the potential benefits outweigh the potential costs. By striking the right balance between innovation and risk-taking, entrepreneurs can create new products and services that have the potential to change the world.

COMMON TRAITS OF SUCCESSFUL ENTREPRENEURS

Successful entrepreneurs possess a wide range of traits that help them succeed in their business ventures. Here are some common traits of successful entrepreneurs:

- **Passion and Perseverance:** Successful entrepreneurs have a deep passion for their business ideas and the drive to pursue them even in the face of challenges and setbacks. They are also persistent and determined to achieve their goals.

- **Creativity and Innovation:** Entrepreneurs are creative thinkers who can generate new ideas and innovative solutions to problems. They are often able to see opportunities where others see obstacles.

- **Risk-taking:** Entrepreneurs are comfortable taking calculated risks and are not afraid to fail. They see failure as an opportunity to learn and grow.

- **Adaptability:** Entrepreneurs need to be flexible and adaptable to changing market conditions and customer needs. They can pivot and adjust their business strategy as needed.

- **Resourcefulness:** Successful entrepreneurs are resourceful and make the most of the resources they have. They are good at finding creative solutions to problems and are willing to do whatever it takes to achieve their goals.

- **Strong Work Ethic:** Entrepreneurs are willing to work hard and put in long hours to achieve their goals. They are often the first ones in and the last ones out.

- **Focus and Discipline:** Successful entrepreneurs focus on their goals and are disciplined in their approach. They prioritize and manage their time effectively.

- **Resilience:** Entrepreneurs need to be resilient and able to bounce back from setbacks and failures. They are able to learn from their mistakes and use those lessons to improve and grow.

Overall, successful entrepreneurs comprise a diverse group of individuals with a variety of skills and traits. The traits listed above are common among many successful entrepreneurs and can be developed through practice and experience.

CLASSICAL DEFINITIONS OF ENTREPRENEURIAL OPPORTUNITIES

Entrepreneurial opportunities are the foundation of entrepreneurship, and their identification and exploitation are essential for the success of any venture. Different scholars have provided various definitions of entrepreneurial opportunities based on their individual perspectives. In this section, we will explore the definitions offered by Carson (1982), Drucker (1985), Baumol (1993), Kirzner (1997), and others.

Carson (1982) defined entrepreneurial opportunities as "potential products or services not currently being offered by established businesses." He emphasized the role of the entrepreneur in identifying and exploiting market gaps by introducing new products or services not currently available in the market. Drucker (1985) defined an entrepreneurial opportunity as "a situation in which a new product, service, raw material, or a production method can be introduced and sold at greater than its cost of production." Drucker's definition highlights the importance of profitability and cost-effectiveness as critical elements of opportunities.

Baumol (1993) defined entrepreneurial opportunities as "instances in which new products, services, raw materials, or production methods can be sold at prices that are higher than their costs." Like Drucker, Baumol emphasizes the profitability aspect of entrepreneurial opportunities. Kirzner (1997) defined entrepreneurial opportunities as "situations where there is an imperfect match between the knowledge of buyers and sellers." In other words, Kirzner emphasized the importance of information asymmetry as a critical element of entrepreneurial opportunities.

Despite the differences in their definitions, these scholars share a common theme: the identification and exploitation of market gaps. They all highlight the importance of the entrepreneur in identifying opportunities and taking action to exploit them. They also emphasize the importance of profitability and cost-effectiveness in evaluating entrepreneurial opportunities.

In conclusion, the definitions of entrepreneurial opportunities provided by Carson (1982), Drucker (1985), Baumol (1993), Kirzner (1997), and others highlight the importance of identifying and exploiting market gaps. These definitions also highlight the importance of profitability and cost-effectiveness as critical elements of entrepreneurial opportunities. Entrepreneurs need to understand the various definitions of entrepreneurial opportunities to identify and exploit them effectively in their ventures.

MODERN INTERPRETATIONS OF ENTREPRENEURIAL OPPORTUNITIES

Various scholars and experts have studied the concept of entrepreneurial opportunities for several decades. However, perspectives on this topic have evolved over time due to the changes in the business environment and the emergence of new theories and practices. In this section, we will discuss the evolving perspectives on entrepreneurial opportunities among current academics and experts.

One of the primary shifts in the perspective on entrepreneurial opportunities has been from a focus on identifying and exploiting existing opportunities to creating and shaping new ones. This shift is reflected in Saras Sarasvathy's effectuation theory, which emphasizes the idea that entrepreneurs do not predict the future but rather shape it by taking action and involving stakeholders in the creation of new opportunities.

Another shift has been toward a more dynamic and process-oriented view of entrepreneurial opportunities. Rather than seeing opportunities as fixed and stable, some scholars now view them as emergent and evolving over time. This perspective is reflected in the concept of "opportunity creation," which suggests that opportunities arise from complex and dynamic interactions between individuals, social networks, and the broader business environment.

In addition, there has been a growing recognition of the role of context in shaping entrepreneurial opportunities. Scholars such as Shane and Venkataraman have emphasized the importance of understanding the social, economic, and institutional context in which opportunities arise. They argue that entrepreneurs need to be aware of the larger systems in which they operate and adapt to changing circumstances to succeed.

Finally, there has been an increasing focus on the importance of social and environmental entrepreneurship. This perspective emphasizes the idea that entrepreneurship can be used to address social and environmental problems and to create economic value. As a result, there has been growing interest in topics such as social innovation, sustainable business practices, and corporate social responsibility.

In conclusion, the perspectives on entrepreneurial opportunities have evolved significantly over time, reflecting changes in the business environment and the emergence of new theories and practices. Today, scholars and experts emphasize the importance of creating and shaping new opportunities, taking a dynamic and process-oriented view of opportunities, understanding the role of context, and addressing social and environmental issues through entrepreneurship.

CURRENT RESEARCH ON ENTREPRENEURIAL OPPORTUNITIES

Entrepreneurial opportunities have been a topic of research for many years, and current studies are expanding the understanding of how these opportunities are identified, evaluated, and pursued. Some of the current research on entrepreneurial opportunities includes the following:

Identification and evaluation of opportunities – Researchers are studying the ways in which entrepreneurs identify and evaluate potential opportunities, including the role of social networks, experience, and cognitive processes in opportunity recognition.

Resource acquisition – Another area of research focuses on how entrepreneurs acquire the resources needed to pursue opportunities, such as funding, human capital, and strategic partnerships.

Technology and innovation – With the rise of technology startups, research is examining the impact of innovation on the identification and pursuit of entrepreneurial opportunities. This includes the use of emerging technologies, such as artificial intelligence and blockchain, to create new business models and disrupt traditional industries.

Social and environmental entrepreneurship – Increasingly, entrepreneurs are focused on creating businesses that have a positive social or environmental impact. Current research explores the motivations and challenges of social and environmental entrepreneurs, as well as the unique opportunities and resources available to them.

Cross-cultural differences – Entrepreneurial opportunities may vary across distinct cultural contexts, and researchers are exploring the ways in which culture and institutions influence the identification and pursuit of opportunities.

Overall, the current research on entrepreneurial opportunities is expanding the understanding of how these opportunities arise, how they are pursued, and their impact on society and the economy. By studying the identification and pursuit of entrepreneurial opportunities, researchers can inform the development of policies and programs that support entrepreneurship and innovation.

EMERGING TRENDS AND OPPORTUNITIES

The field of entrepreneurship is constantly evolving and presents numerous opportunities for those interested in pursuing a career in this area. One of the most significant trends in recent years has been the growth of technology-based products and services. From software and apps to e-commerce platforms and social media, technology has had a profound impact on the way entrepreneurs do business.

One of the most exciting emerging areas in entrepreneurship is artificial intelligence (AI) and machine learning. These technologies have the potential to revolutionize a wide range of industries and have already significantly impacted areas such as healthcare, finance, and transportation. As AI and machine learning become more sophisticated, we can expect to see even more applications in areas such as marketing, customer service, and logistics.

Another emerging area of relevance for young entrepreneurs is data science. With the explosion of digital data, the ability to collect, analyze, and interpret this data has become increasingly important for businesses of all sizes. From predictive analytics to personalized marketing, data science is a powerful tool for entrepreneurs looking to gain a competitive advantage.

In addition to these specific areas of focus, several broader trends are also worth noting. One is the growing emphasis on social responsibility and sustainability. Consumers and investors are increasingly interested in companies that prioritize ethical and sustainable practices, and this presents an opportunity for entrepreneurs to create businesses that align with these values.

Another trend is the growing importance of collaboration and partnerships. With the rise of the gig economy and remote work, entrepreneurs are increasingly turning to partnerships and collaboration to grow their businesses. This can take the form of strategic alliances, joint ventures, or simply sharing resources and expertise.

Overall, there are numerous emerging trends and opportunities in entrepreneurship for young people to consider. While technology-based products and services are an important focus, it is also important to consider broader trends such as social responsibility and collaboration. By staying up to date with these trends and looking for opportunities to innovate, young entrepreneurs can position themselves for success in this exciting and constantly evolving field.

EMERGING OPPORTUNITIES DIFFER FROM TRADITIONAL OPPORTUNITIES

Technological advancements and the widespread availability of digital platforms mark emerging opportunities in entrepreneurship. Compared to traditional entrepreneurial opportunities, these emerging opportunities are more likely to focus on technology-based products and services that leverage the internet, social media, and other digital tools.

One of the most significant differences between traditional and emerging opportunities is the pace of innovation. Technological advancements in fields like artificial intelligence (AI), machine learning, and data science are occurring at a rapid pace, enabling entrepreneurs to leverage these emerging tools to create new and innovative products and services. This contrasts traditional entrepreneurial opportunities, which tend to be based on existing ideas and markets.

Another difference is the focus on scalability. Emerging opportunities often have the potential to scale quickly due to the digital nature of the products and services offered. Digital platforms can reach millions of users, allowing entrepreneurs to leverage economies of scale to grow their businesses rapidly. In contrast, traditional entrepreneurial opportunities tend to be more limited in their scalability, as they are often tied to physical products or services that require a significant investment in infrastructure and personnel to grow.

A third difference is the role of data in decision-making. Emerging opportunities in entrepreneurship often involve the collection and analysis of copious amounts of data, enabling entrepreneurs to make data-driven decisions about their businesses. In contrast, traditional entrepreneurial opportunities are often based more on intuition and market experience, as the data necessary for informed decision-making may not be readily available.

Finally, emerging opportunities in entrepreneurship are often more focused on solving complex problems and meeting unmet needs. This is particularly true in fields like healthcare, education, and environmental sustainability, where technological advancements enable entrepreneurs to tackle some of society's most pressing challenges. Traditional entrepreneurial opportunities tend to be more focused on meeting existing market needs and may not have the same level of social impact.

In summary, emerging opportunities in entrepreneurship are characterized by a focus on technology-based products and services, scalability, data-driven decision-making, and a focus on solving complex problems. These opportunities differ from traditional entrepreneurial opportunities in terms of their pace of innovation, scalability, data focus, and social impact. As such, they represent a unique set of challenges and opportunities for young entrepreneurs looking to build successful businesses in today's digital economy.

LARGE COMPANIES AND ENTREPRENEURIAL OPPORTUNITIES

Large companies can be successful at entrepreneurship by developing new products or services that have the potential to change industries or create new ones. Some examples include the following:

- **Amazon:** Amazon began as an online bookstore in 1994 and has since become a massive online retailer that has expanded into many other areas, including cloud computing, entertainment, and artificial intelligence. One of the most successful initiatives of Amazon has been the development of Amazon Web Services (AWS). AWS is a cloud computing platform that provides a wide range of services, including storage, computing, and databases. AWS has revolutionized the technology industry by enabling small startups and large enterprises to access affordable and scalable computing resources. AWS has helped to make cloud computing a mainstream technology that has become an essential component of modern businesses.

- **Apple:** Apple is known for its innovative products that have transformed the technology industry. One of the most successful initiatives of Apple has been the development of its iPhone. The iPhone was introduced in 2007 and has since become one of the most successful products in history. The iPhone has transformed the mobile phone market and revolutionized the way people communicate and interact with technology. Apple's iPhone was a groundbreaking innovation that combined touchscreens, internet access, cameras, and a wide range of apps that enabled people to do things they had never done before. The success of the iPhone has enabled Apple to become the most valuable company in the world.

- **Google:** Google, originally a search engine, has expanded over the years to include a variety of products and services that have become an integral part of our daily lives. One of the most successful initiatives of Google was developing its Android mobile operating system. Google realized the growing importance of mobile devices and wanted to be a major player in that market. They acquired Android in 2005; since then, it has become the most widely used mobile operating system globally. Android has been instrumental in enabling Google to monetize mobile search compete with Apple's iOS.

These initiatives often require significant investment and risk-taking but can lead to significant rewards for the company and its stakeholders. As such, it is important for companies to invest in innovation and keep an eye out for emerging trends and opportunities.

SUMMARY

This chapter delved into entrepreneurial opportunities, which are at the core of entrepreneurship. The chapter began by defining entrepreneurship as creating value through identifying and exploiting entrepreneurial opportunities. It also discussed the different types of entrepreneurship: startup, social, and intrapreneurship.

Next, the chapter discussed the importance of innovation and risk-taking for both startup entrepreneurs and corporate innovators. Successful entrepreneurs were found to share common traits such as a willingness to take risks, persistence, and the ability to adapt to changing circumstances.

The chapter went on to examine the classical definitions of entrepreneurial opportunities provided by Carson, Drucker, Baumol, Kirzner, and others. Although these definitions varied in some respects, they all emphasized the importance of identifying opportunities in the market and exploiting them to create value.

The chapter then shifted to explore the emerging perspectives on entrepreneurial opportunities among current academics and experts. It examined the evolving trends in entrepreneurship, such as technology-based products, software, apps, artificial intelligence, machine learning, and data science, which present new opportunities for young entrepreneurs.

The chapter provided case studies of successful entrepreneurial initiatives by large companies, including Amazon, Apple, and Google. These case studies demonstrated how large companies embrace entrepreneurial opportunities to remain competitive in the market.

In summary, this chapter underscored the significance of identifying and exploiting entrepreneurial opportunities. It also highlighted the need for innovation and risk-taking, the common traits of successful entrepreneurs, and the different types of entrepreneurship. Additionally, it provided an overview of the classical definitions of entrepreneurial opportunities, emerging trends, current research, and case studies of successful entrepreneurial initiatives by large companies.

4. Strategic Decision-Making

When you're first thinking through an idea, it's important not to get bogged down in complexity.

Thinking simply and clearly is hard to do.

Richard Branson

Founder of Virgin Group

The Importance of Strategic Decision-making in Entrepreneurship

Strategic decision-making is a crucial aspect of entrepreneurship, enabling entrepreneurs to identify and seize new opportunities, navigate risks and uncertainties, and achieve their long-term goals. In a constantly evolving business landscape where disruptive technologies and emerging trends can quickly make existing business models obsolete, entrepreneurs need to make strategic decisions that are adaptable, innovative, and forward-looking.

Entrepreneurs face numerous strategic decisions that are often difficult and complex, including deciding which products or services to offer, which target market to focus on, and how to allocate resources effectively. These decisions require a deep understanding of the market, competition, customers, and internal capabilities. Entrepreneurs must evaluate the risks and rewards of different alternatives and choose the best course of action that aligns with their business objectives.

Strategic decision-making is also essential for entrepreneurs to maintain their competitive edge and sustain their growth over time. Effective decision-making enables entrepreneurs to anticipate potential challenges and develop proactive mitigation strategies. Strategic decision-making also helps entrepreneurs identify opportunities for growth and expansion, such as expanding their product lines, entering new markets, or exploring partnerships and collaborations.

Another crucial aspect of strategic decision-making is the ability to think creatively and innovatively. Entrepreneurs must be able to challenge conventional wisdom, think outside the box, and explore new approaches and ideas that can help them differentiate themselves from their competitors. Successful entrepreneurs have taken bold strategic decisions that have transformed their businesses and disrupted their industries.

In summary, strategic decision-making is a critical aspect of entrepreneurship. It enables entrepreneurs to navigate the complexities of the business landscape, seize new opportunities, manage risks, and achieve their long-term goals. Entrepreneurs skilled in strategic decision-making are more likely to succeed and thrive in a rapidly changing environment.

STRATEGIC DECISION-MAKING IN ENTREPRENEURSHIP

Strategic decision-making is a process of selecting the most appropriate course of action for a business to achieve its long-term goals and objectives. This type of decision-making requires a comprehensive understanding of the business environment, including internal and external factors, to identify opportunities, threats, strengths, and weaknesses. Strategic decision-making involves analyzing and evaluating diverse options to determine the most effective approach to achieving the desired outcome.

Strategic decisions often involve high levels of uncertainty and risk and require a significant investment of time and resources. They are typically made by top-level executives and stakeholders, who are responsible for setting the direction of the business and making decisions that will have a long-term impact on the organization.

Strategic decision-making is crucial for identifying and pursuing opportunities that will help the business achieve sustainable growth and success. Entrepreneurs must be able to make informed decisions based on a comprehensive understanding of their business environment and must be able to balance short-term needs with long-term goals.

THE CHALLENGES OF STRATEGIC DECISION-MAKING FOR ENTREPRENEURS

Strategic decision-making is a critical component of entrepreneurship, as entrepreneurs are constantly faced with tough decisions that can have significant consequences for their ventures. In an entrepreneurial context, strategic decision-making refers to the process of identifying and evaluating alternatives to guide the growth and development of a new venture. This can include decisions about product development, market entry, resource allocation, and partnerships, among others.

Entrepreneurial decision-making can be characterized as a highly dynamic process where entrepreneurs must constantly adapt to changing market conditions, resource constraints, and customer feedback. As such, effective strategic decision-making requires anticipating and responding to changes in the external environment. This means that entrepreneurs must be highly attuned to customer needs, competitor strategies, and broader market trends to identify new opportunities and mitigate potential risks.

Another important aspect of strategic decision-making in entrepreneurship is the need to balance risk and reward. Successful entrepreneurs are typically risk-takers, but they must also be able to assess and manage risk effectively. This involves carefully considering the potential benefits and drawbacks of various strategic options and a realistic assessment of the resources and capabilities required to execute them.

Finally, strategic decision-making in entrepreneurship is also heavily influenced by cognitive biases and heuristics. Entrepreneurs often rely on mental shortcuts and quick judgments when making decisions, leading to errors in judgment and suboptimal outcomes. Effective strategic decision-making requires the ability to recognize and overcome these biases and to gather and analyze data rigorously and systematically.

Overall, strategic decision-making is a critical element of entrepreneurship, enabling entrepreneurs to navigate the uncertainties and challenges of launching and growing a new venture. By taking a deliberate and thoughtful approach to decision-making, entrepreneurs can increase their chances of success and create sustainable value for their customers, employees, and investors.

OVERVIEW OF THE STRATEGIC DECISION-MAKING PROCESS

The strategic decision-making process is a systematic approach to making choices about the direction and objectives of an organization or a venture. The process typically involves a series of steps that help to ensure that decisions are made based on the best available information, and that all relevant factors are taken into account.

The following are the key steps involved in the strategic decision-making process:

1. **Identifying the Problem or Opportunity:** This is the initial step in the decision-making process, where the entrepreneur identifies a problem or opportunity that needs to be addressed. This could involve an issue that needs to be solved or an opportunity to exploit.

45

2. **Gathering Information:** Once the problem or opportunity has been identified, the entrepreneur must gather relevant information. This may involve collecting data, conducting market research, or seeking expert advice.

3. **Generating Alternatives:** The entrepreneur needs to generate a range of alternatives based on the information collected. This could involve developing different business models, identifying potential partners, or exploring various market segments.

4. **Evaluating Alternatives:** In this step, the entrepreneur needs to evaluate the various alternatives against a set of criteria. This could include financial criteria, such as revenue and profit, as well as non-financial criteria, such as social impact and environmental sustainability.

5. **Selecting the Best Alternative:** Once the alternatives have been evaluated, the entrepreneur needs to choose the best option. This involves weighing up the pros and cons of each option and making a decision based on the criteria that have been established.

6. **Implementing the Decision:** The final step in the decision-making process is to implement the chosen alternative. This may involve developing a business plan, securing funding, and putting in place the necessary resources to execute the plan.

Throughout the strategic decision-making process, it's important for entrepreneurs to be flexible and adaptive. This is because the decision-making process is not always linear, and entrepreneurs may need to revise their decisions based on changing circumstances or new information that comes to light.

COGNITION AND ENTREPRENEURSHIP

Cognition refers to the mental processes and activities that involve acquiring, processing, storing, and using information. It is a broad term encompassing all mental processes and activities occurring within the brain, including perception, attention, memory, reasoning, problem-solving, and decision-making. Cognition plays a critical role in the decision-making process as it enables individuals to evaluate different alternatives, assess risks, and determine the potential outcomes of their decisions.

In decision-making, cognition involves using mental processes and activities to assess information, generate and evaluate alternatives, and select the best course of action. It is essential for entrepreneurs to have a deep understanding of the cognitive processes involved in decision-making, as the effectiveness of their decision-making will directly impact the success of their ventures.

Cognitive processes such as attention and perception help entrepreneurs to identify and analyze information relevant to their decision-making. Memory plays a vital role in retaining and recalling information, which is necessary for making informed decisions. Reasoning and problem-solving are also critical cognitive processes that are involved in generating and evaluating different alternatives.

Entrepreneurs must be aware of potential biases and limitations in their cognitive processes. For example, individuals often tend to overestimate the likelihood of positive outcomes and underestimate the likelihood of negative outcomes. This can lead to decision-making that is not based on a realistic assessment of the situation. Similarly, individuals may have a bias towards options that are familiar or have worked in the past, which can limit their ability to consider novel or innovative solutions.

In summary, cognition is a critical component of the decision-making process, and entrepreneurs must be aware of the cognitive processes involved in their decision-making. By understanding these processes, entrepreneurs can make informed decisions that will lead to the success of their ventures.

CONNECTION BETWEEN COGNITION AND THE ENTREPRENEURIAL PROCESS

Cognition is the mental process of acquiring knowledge and understanding through thought, experience, and the senses. In the context of decision-making, cognition is the way in which an individual perceives, processes, and interprets information to arrive at a decision.

Entrepreneurship involves making decisions with high levels of uncertainty and risk. Thus, cognition plays a crucial role in the entrepreneurial process. Entrepreneurs need to process and interpret information from various sources to make decisions that can affect the future of their businesses. They also need to be able to identify patterns and trends in complex and ambiguous situations to make sense of the information available.

One way cognition influences the entrepreneurial process is by identifying and evaluating opportunities. Entrepreneurs need to be able to recognize and evaluate opportunities that may not be immediately apparent to others. This requires cognitive processes such as pattern recognition, the ability to connect seemingly unrelated information, and the ability to generate novel solutions to problems.

Cognition also influences the way entrepreneurs approach risk. Risk perception is subjective and varies from person to person. Entrepreneurs with a high risk tolerance may be more likely to pursue opportunities that others might view as too risky. The ability to accurately assess and manage risk is critical to the success of any entrepreneurial venture.

Another important aspect of cognition in the entrepreneurial process is the ability to learn from experience. Entrepreneurs need to be able to reflect on past experiences and learn from their mistakes. This requires cognitive processes such as self-awareness and metacognition, which is the ability to think about one's own thinking.

Finally, cognition is important in the development of strategies and plans. Entrepreneurs need to be able to analyze and interpret information to develop a strategic plan that will guide their business. This requires cognitive processes such as problem-solving, decision-making, and generating creative solutions to complex problems.

In summary, cognition is a crucial component of the entrepreneurial process. Entrepreneurs need to be able to identify and evaluate opportunities, assess, and manage risk, learn from experience, and develop strategies and plans. The ability to think critically, creatively, and adaptively is essential for success in entrepreneurship.

THE IMPACT OF COGNITIVE BIASES ON DECISION-MAKING

Cognitive biases are systematic errors in thinking and decision-making that are caused by our brain's tendency to simplify complex situations by relying on mental shortcuts. While often helpful in processing information quickly, these mental shortcuts or heuristics can sometimes lead to errors in judgment and decision-making. In the context of entrepreneurship, cognitive biases can significantly impact the decision-making process and lead to poor outcomes.

One common cognitive bias that can impact entrepreneurship is confirmation bias. This bias occurs when entrepreneurs seek out information confirming their existing beliefs or assumptions, while ignoring or discounting information that challenges them. This can lead to a narrow and incomplete view of a situation, resulting in missed opportunities or poor decisions.

Another common cognitive bias is the sunk cost fallacy, which occurs when entrepreneurs continue to invest in a project or idea despite evidence suggesting that it will not be successful. This bias can lead to a loss of resources and time, preventing entrepreneurs from recognizing when it is time to move on from a project.

Overconfidence bias is another cognitive bias that can impact entrepreneurs. This bias occurs when entrepreneurs overestimate their own abilities or the likelihood of success, which can lead to overinvestment in a project, underestimation of risks, and ultimately failure.

To avoid these cognitive biases, entrepreneurs should take steps to increase their awareness of them and actively work to mitigate their effects. This includes seeking out diverse perspectives, challenging assumptions, and making decisions based on objective data and evidence rather than personal biases. Additionally, entrepreneurs can employ tools such as decision matrices and scenario planning to help ensure they consider multiple options and potential outcomes.

HOW TO NAVIGATE THE STRATEGIC DECISION-MAKING PROCESS

Step 1. Recognition of a Problem

The first step in the strategic decision-making process is to recognize that there is a problem or opportunity. This recognition is the starting point for any decision-making process, and it is essential for entrepreneurs to be able to identify and define the problem they are trying to solve or the opportunity they are trying to pursue.

Recognizing a problem or opportunity requires careful observation, analysis, and an understanding of the market and industry trends. It is important to identify the root cause of the problem rather than just addressing the symptoms. Entrepreneurs must be able to recognize patterns and trends in the market and understand how these trends will affect their business in the future.

In recognizing a problem or opportunity, entrepreneurs should ask themselves several questions: What is the current market situation? What problems are customers facing? What are the gaps in the market that can be filled? What trends are emerging in the industry? What are the competitive pressures? By answering these questions, entrepreneurs can identify opportunities for innovation and growth.

51

Entrepreneurs should also consider the impact of their decision on their business, customers, and stakeholders. They should analyze the potential risks and rewards of pursuing a particular course of action. By recognizing a problem or opportunity, entrepreneurs can begin the process of developing a strategic plan to address the issue and achieve their goals.

In addition, it is important to note that recognizing a problem or opportunity is not a one-time event. Entrepreneurs must constantly monitor the market and be aware of changes in the industry. They should be receptive to feedback from customers and stakeholders and use this information to refine their strategy. By staying aware of changes in the market and industry, entrepreneurs can identify new opportunities and adjust their strategy accordingly.

Step 2. Generation of Alternatives

The second step in the strategic decision-making process is generating alternatives. After entrepreneurs recognize a problem, they need to identify and consider various alternatives to address it. Generating alternative solutions is critical because it allows entrepreneurs to explore various options and compare their benefits and drawbacks.

Generating alternatives is a major step in the decision-making process because it provides a foundation for evaluating options and selecting the best solution. Entrepreneurs who do not generate enough alternatives may be unable to identify the optimal solution, leading to a suboptimal outcome. On the other hand, generating too many alternatives can lead to decision paralysis, where the entrepreneur becomes overwhelmed with options and struggles to make a decision.

Entrepreneurs can use various techniques to generate alternatives, such as brainstorming, mind mapping, and analyzing strengths, weaknesses, opportunities, and threats associated with each alternative (SWOT analysis). Brainstorming is a popular technique that involves generating ideas in a group setting, while mind mapping involves creating a visual representation of various ideas and how they relate to each other. During this stage, it is important to remain open to all possibilities, even if some alternatives may initially seem unlikely or impractical. The goal is to generate a wide range of options that can be evaluated against specific criteria to determine the best solution.

Ensuring that the alternatives generated align with the entrepreneur's mission, vision, and values is also important. An alternative that does not align with these foundational elements may not be a suitable choice, even if it appears to be the most practical option.

Ultimately, the goal of generating alternatives is to have a diverse set of options that can be compared and evaluated in the next step of the strategic decision-making process.

Step 3. Evaluation of Alternatives

The third step in the strategic decision-making process is to evaluate alternatives. After identifying possible solutions, the next step is to evaluate their strengths and weaknesses in relation to the criteria set in the first step. This step is crucial because it involves weighing the pros and cons of each option, considering their feasibility, practicality, and potential impact.

To evaluate alternatives, entrepreneurs use a variety of tools and techniques, such as decision matrices, cost-benefit analyses, and scenario analyses. These tools help quantify each alternative's advantages and disadvantages, determine each option's risks and rewards, and predict the potential outcomes of each course of action. In some cases, entrepreneurs may also seek advice from experts, consultants, or trusted advisors to help them evaluate alternatives and provide additional perspectives.

One common method used to evaluate alternatives is the decision matrix. A decision matrix is a tool that helps to organize and evaluate different alternatives based on various criteria. To use a decision matrix, entrepreneurs typically create a table with the alternatives listed across the top and the evaluation criteria on the left side. They then assign weights to each criterion based on its importance and rate each alternative on a scale of 1 to 10 for each criterion. The resulting scores can then be added to determine the most favorable alternative.

Another method used to evaluate alternatives is scenario analysis. Scenario analysis involves creating different potential future scenarios based on various assumptions and then evaluating each alternative under each scenario. This method is useful for evaluating alternatives in uncertain or unpredictable environments, as it allows entrepreneurs to consider a range of possible outcomes and prepare for different eventualities.

Overall, evaluating alternatives is an important step in the strategic decision-making process because it helps entrepreneurs make informed decisions based on a thorough assessment of each option's potential risks and benefits. By using tools such as decision matrices and scenario analyses, entrepreneurs can evaluate alternatives more objectively and identify the best course of action for their venture.

Step 4. Selection of the Best Alternative

The final step of the strategic decision-making process is selecting the best alternative. After identifying the problem, generating alternatives, and evaluating them, the entrepreneur must choose the one that best meets their evaluation criteria. It is essential to recognize that this step is the culmination of the entire decision-making process and the one with the most significant impact on the entrepreneur's success.

One of the critical factors in selecting the best alternative is the decision-making process's effectiveness in identifying the best option. While it may seem straightforward, choosing the best alternative can be challenging for entrepreneurs. Often, they will face multiple equally compelling alternatives or must choose between an option with higher financial returns and one that aligns better with their values.

The entrepreneur's selection process requires a well-defined evaluation criterion, which is the standard against which each alternative is judged. For instance, if the evaluation criterion is profitability, the entrepreneur must select the alternative that provides the most financial gain. The entrepreneur must ensure the evaluation criterion aligns with the overall goals and values of the enterprise.

The selection of the best alternative may also require the entrepreneur to consider the potential risks and challenges that come with the decision. They must be prepared to identify and manage these challenges. The entrepreneur may consider how they will mitigate the risks or identify alternative strategies to address them.

It is also essential to have the necessary resources to implement the chosen alternative. This may include financial resources, human resources, and infrastructure. If the entrepreneur cannot obtain the necessary resources, they may need to revise their choice and select an alternative that better aligns with the resources available.

In summary, the final step of the strategic decision-making process requires the entrepreneur to choose the alternative that best meets their evaluation criteria. This step is critical to the overall success of the enterprise and requires careful consideration of the evaluation criteria, potential risks, and available resources.

EXAMPLES OF SUCCESSFUL STRATEGIC DECISION-MAKING IN ENTREPRENEURSHIP

There are a number of terrific examples of successful strategic decision-making from startups that became big companies, including:

- **Airbnb:** Airbnb, the online marketplace for short-term lodging, was founded in 2008 by Brian Chesky, Joe Gebbia, and Nathan Blecharczyk. The founders recognized a problem with the hotel industry and saw an opportunity to provide an alternative that was more personal and cost-effective. They generated several alternatives, including a bed and breakfast service and a community travel guide, but ultimately decided on an online platform that allows individuals to rent out their homes. Airbnb was able to evaluate alternatives and select the best option, which has disrupted the hospitality industry. By creating a user-friendly platform and focusing on customer experience, Airbnb achieved significant growth and expanded its services to other areas, including experiences and luxury accommodations.
- **Tesla:** Tesla, the electric vehicle and clean energy company, was founded in 2003 by Elon Musk. The founder recognized a problem with the transportation industry and saw an opportunity to provide a sustainable and innovative solution. They generated several alternatives, including a high-

performance electric sports car and a mass-market electric vehicle, but ultimately decided on a strategy that focused on developing a sustainable energy ecosystem. Tesla was able to evaluate their alternatives and select the best option, which has disrupted the automotive industry. By leveraging technology and focusing on sustainability, Tesla achieved significant growth and expanded its services to other areas, including solar energy and battery storage.

- **Uber:** Uber, the ride-hailing service, was founded in 2009 and has since become one of the world's most successful and innovative companies. The founders, Travis Kalanick and Garrett Camp, recognized a problem with the taxi industry and saw an opportunity to provide a better solution. They generated several alternatives, including limousine and courier services, but ultimately decided on a ride-sharing service. Uber was able to evaluate their alternatives and select the best option, revolutionizing the transportation industry. By leveraging technology and a flexible workforce, Uber has been able to achieve exponential growth and expand its services to other areas, including food delivery and freight.

In each of these examples, the entrepreneurs recognized a problem and saw an opportunity to provide a better solution. They generated several alternatives, evaluated their options, and selected the best alternative. By focusing on customer experience, leveraging technology, and managing risk, these entrepreneurs achieved significant growth and disrupted their respective industries. They demonstrate that strategic decision-making is critical for success in entrepreneurship.

SUMMARY

This chapter focuses on strategic decision-making in entrepreneurship. The chapter provides an overview of the strategic decision-making process, which includes recognizing problems, generating alternatives, evaluating alternatives, and selecting the best alternative.

The chapter emphasizes the importance of strategic decision-making in entrepreneurship, as it can significantly impact a venture's success or failure. Furthermore, the chapter explores the concept of cognition and its connection to the entrepreneurial process. It also highlights the importance of recognizing cognitive biases, which can impact decision-making.

The first step in the strategic decision-making process is recognizing problems. Entrepreneurs recognize problems by scanning the environment for opportunities or threats. It is important for entrepreneurs to recognize problems because it allows them to generate alternative solutions.

The second step in the strategic decision-making process is generating alternatives. Entrepreneurs generate alternatives through creativity, and it is important to consider both short-term and long-term consequences when generating alternatives.

The third step in the strategic decision-making process is evaluating alternatives. Entrepreneurs evaluate alternatives through objective analysis and consider factors such as feasibility, acceptability, and vulnerability.

The fourth and final step in the strategic decision-making process is selecting the best alternative. Entrepreneurs select the best alternative by considering the risks associated with each alternative and taking steps to mitigate those risks.

The chapter also includes three case studies that illustrate successful strategic decision-making in entrepreneurship. These case studies demonstrate the importance of recognizing problems, generating alternatives, and evaluating alternatives in the strategic decision-making process.

In summary, the chapter emphasizes the importance of strategic decision-making in entrepreneurship and provides a framework for the strategic decision-making process. The chapter highlights the role of cognition in the entrepreneurial process and the importance of objective analysis and risk management in evaluating and selecting alternatives. Finally, the case studies illustrate the practical application of the strategic decision-making process in successful entrepreneurial ventures.

5. Thinking Entrepreneurially

I knew that if I failed, I wouldn't regret that,
but I knew the one thing I might regret is not trying.

Jeff Bezos

Founder of Amazon

With an appreciation for the opportunities and challenges of strategic decision-making, you can explore the next chapters on *entrepreneurial mindset, entrepreneurial motivation,* and *entrepreneurial behavior* as the first three steps of The Opportunity Analysis Canvas.

The Opportunity Analysis Canvas

Emphasis on "Part I – Thinking Entrepreneurially"

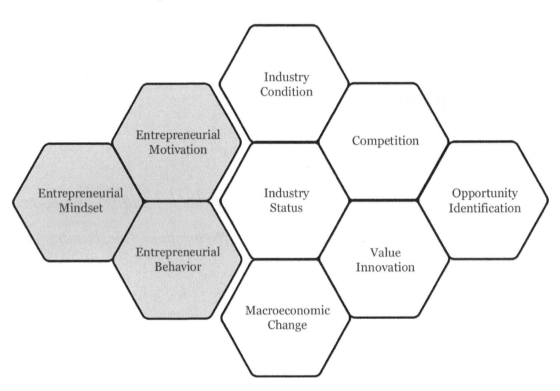

6. Entrepreneurial Mindset

An entrepreneurial mindset is a way of life.
It's about thinking critically, taking calculated risks, and
being persistent in the face of obstacles.

Elon Musk
Founder of Tesla and SpaceX
Co-founder of PayPal

In the world of entrepreneurship, success is often determined by the entrepreneur's mindset. Entrepreneurs are independent individuals deeply committed to persevering in starting and growing a venture. They are typically optimistic and strive for success in their for-profit, non-profit, or social ventures. Entrepreneurs often have a competitive desire to excel and use failure not as a referendum but as a learning tool. While every entrepreneur is unique, they share certain commonalities in their mindset. This chapter focuses on the entrepreneurial mindset, with attention to five key characteristics: achievement, individualism, control, focus, and optimism.

Entrepreneurial mindset refers to a specific way of thinking that allows entrepreneurs to identify opportunities and take risks to pursue them. This mindset is characterized by a powerful desire to achieve and succeed, as well as a willingness to take calculated risks. This mindset allows entrepreneurs to see opportunities where others might see only challenges or obstacles.

While every entrepreneur is unique, there are select commonalities in the entrepreneurial mindset that they share. This chapter focuses on that entrepreneurial mindset with attention to the five characteristics: *achievement, individualism, control, focus,* and *optimism.*

The Opportunity Analysis Canvas

Emphasis on "Entrepreneurial Mindset"

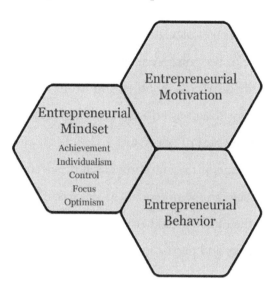

1. The first characteristic of the entrepreneurial mindset is the need for achievement. Entrepreneurs are driven by a desire to achieve something meaningful, to make an impact in the world, and to leave a legacy. They are not content with the status quo and are constantly seeking ways to improve their lives and the lives of others. The pursuit of achievement motivates entrepreneurs to take risks and to persist in the face of obstacles.

2. Individualism is another key characteristic of the entrepreneurial mindset. Entrepreneurs are independent thinkers who are not afraid to challenge conventional wisdom. They have a strong sense of self-reliance and self-confidence, and they trust their own judgment over the opinions of others. This individualism allows entrepreneurs to see the world in a unique way and to identify opportunities that others might overlook.

67

3. Control is a third characteristic of the entrepreneurial mindset. Entrepreneurs have a strong desire to control their own destinies and to be their own bosses. They are not content with working for others and prefer to take control of their own lives. This desire for control motivates entrepreneurs to start their own businesses and take calculated risks to achieve their goals.

4. Focus is a fourth characteristic of the entrepreneurial mindset. Entrepreneurs have a laser-like focus on their goals and are not easily distracted by other opportunities or challenges. They can identify what is most important and prioritize their efforts accordingly. This focus allows entrepreneurs to stay on track and persevere in the face of adversity.

5. Optimism is the final characteristic of the entrepreneurial mindset. Entrepreneurs are typically optimistic individuals who believe in the potential for success. They view failure as a learning tool rather than a referendum on their abilities and are resilient in the face of setbacks. This optimism allows entrepreneurs to take risks and persist in the face of adversity.

In conclusion, the entrepreneurial mindset is a critical component of success in entrepreneurship. The five key characteristics of the entrepreneurial mindset are achievement, individualism, control, focus, and optimism. Entrepreneurs who possess these characteristics are more likely to identify opportunities, take calculated risks, and persist in the face of obstacles. Aspiring entrepreneurs who develop an entrepreneurial mindset will be better equipped to identify and pursue opportunities and navigate the challenges of starting and growing a venture.

Need for Achievement

The need for achievement is a key characteristic of the entrepreneurial mindset. It refers to an individual's desire to set and accomplish challenging goals, take calculated risks, and strive for excellence in their endeavors. Aspiring entrepreneurs with a high need for achievement are driven by the desire to create something meaningful and impactful and are not satisfied with just meeting minimum standards or maintaining the status quo. They constantly seek ways to improve, innovate, and grow their ventures.

The need for achievement is important for aspiring entrepreneurs because it provides the motivation and drive necessary to take on the challenges and uncertainties of entrepreneurship. Starting and growing a venture requires a great deal of effort, persistence, and resilience, as well as the willingness to take risks and make tough decisions. Entrepreneurs with a high need for achievement are more likely to possess these qualities and overcome obstacles and setbacks.

Moreover, the need for achievement is closely tied to the desire for autonomy and independence, which are also important characteristics of the entrepreneurial mindset. Entrepreneurs want to be in control of their own destiny, make their own decisions, and be responsible for the success of their ventures. The need for achievement provides the drive and focus necessary to pursue these goals and create a sense of personal fulfillment and accomplishment.

Finally, the need for achievement is also important for the long-term success of an entrepreneurial venture. Entrepreneurs constantly striving for excellence and looking for ways to improve are more likely to develop innovative products or services, build strong customer relationships, and create a competitive advantage in the marketplace. This can lead to increased revenue, profitability, growth, and the ability to attract and retain top talent and investors.

Overall, the need for achievement is a critical component of the entrepreneurial mindset, providing the motivation, drive, and focus necessary for aspiring entrepreneurs to start and grow successful ventures.

How Do You Know if You Have a High Need for Achievement?

Individuals with a high need for achievement tend to exhibit a number of specific characteristics, behaviors, and attitudes. Here are a few signs that may suggest that you have a high need for achievement:

You set challenging goals for yourself: People with a high need for achievement tend to set difficult and ambitious goals for themselves. They are driven by the desire to achieve something significant and challenging.

You work hard and persist even in the face of obstacles. High achievers tend to work hard and persist even when encountering difficulties and setbacks. They are committed to their goals and are willing to put in the effort required to achieve them.

You are highly self-motivated. Individuals with a high need for achievement tend to be highly self-motivated. They are not dependent on others to motivate them or provide them with direction.
You are goal-oriented: People with a high need for achievement tend to be very goal-oriented. They set clear and specific goals for themselves and work towards achieving them.

You seek feedback and strive for continuous improvement: High achievers tend to be open to feedback and use it to improve their performance. They are not afraid to admit mistakes and learn from them.

You enjoy competition: Individuals with a high need for achievement tend to enjoy competition and are motivated by the desire to outperform others.

You are willing to take calculated risks: High achievers tend to be willing to take calculated risks. They are not reckless, but they are willing to take on challenges and pursue opportunities that have the potential for significant rewards.

Having a high need for achievement can be a valuable asset for aspiring entrepreneurs. It can help them to set ambitious goals, work hard and persist in the face of challenges, and continuously strive for improvement. It can also help them to be self-motivated and goal-oriented and to be willing to take calculated risks to pursue opportunities.

Individualism

Individualism is a characteristic of an entrepreneurial mindset that refers to the desire for independence and the pursuit of personal goals. Entrepreneurs who score high in individualism value their independence and autonomy and have a keen sense of self-direction. They prefer to work alone or with a small group of trusted individuals and often rely on their own skills and abilities to achieve their goals.

Individualism is important for aspiring entrepreneurs because it can help them take risks, be creative, and pursue their ideas without fear of judgment or criticism. Highly individualistic entrepreneurs are more likely to develop unique and innovative products or services, and they are better able to adapt to changes in the market or in their business environment. They are also more likely to persevere in the face of obstacles, setbacks, or failure because they have a powerful sense of personal responsibility and accountability.

Entrepreneurs who score high in individualism are often characterized as self-starters who are comfortable taking risks and making decisions independently. They are confident in their own abilities and are not afraid to challenge conventional wisdom or try something new. They also tend to have a high tolerance for ambiguity and can easily navigate uncertainty and complexity.

Individualism is important for entrepreneurs because it allows them to focus on their vision and pursue their goals with passion and dedication. It also allows them to be more flexible and adaptable in the face of changing circumstances. However, it is important for entrepreneurs to recognize the limitations of individualism and seek out support and feedback from others when needed. Collaboration and teamwork are essential for success in many entrepreneurial ventures, and entrepreneurs who are too focused on individualism may miss valuable opportunities to learn and grow.

WHY COLLECTIVISM IS VALUABLE FOR ASPIRING ENTREPRENEURS

Collectivism is the belief that the group is more important than the individual, and that the needs and goals of the group should take precedence over the needs and goals of any individual member. In a collectivist society, people tend to identify closely with the group to which they belong, such as their family, community, or country. They place a high value on social harmony, interdependence, and the common good.

While individualism is often associated with entrepreneurship, collectivism can also be important for aspiring entrepreneurs, especially in certain cultural contexts. In some societies, the group is highly valued, and individuals are expected to place the needs of the group above their own personal ambitions. In these cultures, entrepreneurs may need to balance their desire for personal success with the needs and expectations of the larger community.

In addition, many successful businesses are built on strong relationships and partnerships with others, such as co-founders, employees, suppliers, and customers. As such, a collectivist mindset that values collaboration, trust, and teamwork can be highly beneficial for entrepreneurs who seek to build successful ventures.

INDIVIDUALISM VERSUS COLLECTIVISM

Individualism and collectivism are two distinct cultural orientations that define a person's inclination towards individual or group goals. While individualists prioritize personal achievements and success, collectivists value cooperation, relationships, and group harmony.

To determine if you are more individualistic or collectivistic, consider your values, beliefs, and behaviors. Individualistic people typically prioritize their autonomy, independence, and personal achievement. They prefer to work alone, take risks, and make decisions based on their own criteria. They value competition and are motivated by self-interest.

On the other hand, collectivistic individuals emphasize social norms, community values, and the well-being of their group. They prefer to work in teams, avoid confrontation, and make decisions based on group consensus. They value cooperation and are motivated by group interests.

You can also assess your individualism or collectivism by examining your cultural background, social environment, and personal experiences. For instance, individuals from Western cultures are more likely to be individualistic, whereas those from Eastern cultures are more likely to be collectivistic. Similarly, your family, friends, and community can influence your inclination towards individualism or collectivism. Individual experiences like education, travel, and exposure to different cultures, can also shape your values and beliefs.

It's important to note that individualism and collectivism are not mutually exclusive, and individuals can have varying degrees of both orientations depending on the context and situation. Understanding your cultural orientation can help you recognize your strengths and weaknesses as an entrepreneur and develop effective strategies for achieving your goals.

Control

Locus of control is a psychological concept that refers to an individual's belief about the underlying causes of their experiences and the degree to which they feel they can control those experiences. Individuals with an internal locus of control believe that they have control over the outcomes of their actions and tend to attribute their successes and failures to their own efforts and abilities. On the other hand, individuals with an external locus of control tend to believe that external factors, such as luck or other people's actions, are responsible for their outcomes.

Having an internal locus of control can be highly beneficial for aspiring entrepreneurs. This belief in personal control and responsibility can lead to a stronger sense of self-efficacy, which is the belief in one's ability to succeed in a particular domain.

Entrepreneurs with an internal locus of control tend to be more resilient and persistent, despite setbacks and failures. They are more likely to take ownership of their successes and failures and to use failure as a learning opportunity.

Conversely, entrepreneurs with an external locus of control may struggle to take ownership of their outcomes and persist in the face of challenges. They may be more likely to give up or to blame external factors for their failures, which can hinder their ability to learn from those experiences and adapt their approach.

To determine whether you have an internal or external locus of control, reflect on how you tend to explain your experiences. Do you tend to attribute your successes and failures to your own efforts and abilities, or to external factors beyond your control? Do you feel a sense of control over your life and your outcomes, or do you feel that you are at the mercy of external circumstances? By considering these questions, you can gain insight into your own locus of control and how it may influence your entrepreneurial mindset.

HOW TO KNOW YOUR OWN LOCUS OF CONTROL

Locus of control is a concept used to describe the extent to which individuals believe they have control over the events that affect their lives. In other words, it refers to the degree to which individuals believe they can influence the outcomes of their actions. There are two types of loci of control: internal and external.

To determine your locus of control, you can take a simple questionnaire to help you understand your beliefs about your ability to control your own life. You can find these questionnaires online or in self-help books. The questionnaires typically ask you a series of questions about your beliefs and attitudes towards different situations, and your responses are then used to determine whether you have an internal or external locus of control.

It is important for aspiring entrepreneurs to understand their locus of control because it can impact their ability to take risks and to persist in the face of adversity. Those with a strong internal locus of control are more likely to take initiative and to persist in the face of obstacles, which are important qualities for success as an entrepreneur.

Focus

In the context of entrepreneurship, focus is a state of mind where an entrepreneur is deeply immersed in their work, giving it their undivided attention and effort. It involves a conscious effort to prioritize work, allocate time and resources, and concentrate on the most critical tasks that contribute to the success of the venture. Entrepreneurs who have a strong focus are driven by their vision and goals, and they have a clear idea of what they want to achieve and how to get there.

Our definition of focus in this context is concentration on a specific issue or task. To really focus, you need self-discipline and motivation. Successful entrepreneurs can focus on a task and see it through to completion or to its next milestone. They can be more efficient and do things better by giving tasks their full attention and processing information efficiently and thoroughly. This enables them to be decisive and thoughtful in their decisions.

One of the key aspects of focus is the ability to identify and prioritize the most important tasks. This requires understanding the business and its objectives and thoroughly analyzing available resources. Entrepreneurs with a strong focus know how to leverage their skills, knowledge, and networks to achieve their goals. They can manage their time effectively and avoid distractions that can derail their progress.

The ability to focus is important for aspiring entrepreneurs for several reasons. First, starting a new venture can be overwhelming, and entrepreneurs need to be able to manage their time and resources effectively. Having a clear focus helps entrepreneurs prioritize their tasks and avoid distractions, allowing them to progress towards their goals.

Second, focus is essential for effective decision-making. Entrepreneurs face many choices and opportunities, and having a clear focus helps them evaluate the potential benefits and risks of each option. A focused entrepreneur can make informed decisions and take calculated risks that align with their vision and goals.

Finally, focus is important for maintaining motivation and momentum. Starting a new venture can be challenging, and entrepreneurs often face setbacks and obstacles along the way. A strong focus helps entrepreneurs stay motivated and resilient in the face of these challenges, allowing them to maintain momentum and make progress toward their goals.

To know if you have a strong focus as an entrepreneur, you can ask yourself several questions. Do you have an unclouded vision and mission for your venture? Are you able to prioritize your tasks and manage your time effectively? Can you avoid distractions and maintain your momentum even in the face of setbacks and obstacles? If you can answer yes to these questions, you likely have a strong focus, which is an essential trait for entrepreneurial success.

Ten Ways to Improve Your Focus

1. **Set Clear Goals**: Setting clear and specific goals can help you focus on what you need to accomplish. Make sure to prioritize your goals and break them down into smaller, manageable tasks.

2. **Create a Schedule**: A schedule can help you stay on track and avoid distractions. Block out specific times in your day for different tasks and set specific deadlines for each.

3. **Eliminate Distractions**: Identify the sources of distraction in your environment and remove them. This could include closing unnecessary tabs on your computer or working in a quiet space.

4. **Practice Mindfulness**: Mindfulness is the practice of being present in the moment. Focusing on the task at hand can improve your ability to concentrate and stay focused.

5. **Take Breaks**: Taking breaks can help you recharge and refocus. Make sure to take short breaks throughout the day to avoid burnout.

6. **Exercise**: Exercise can help improve focus by reducing stress and increasing blood flow to the brain.

7. **Use Tools**: Several tools are available to help you improve your focus, such as productivity apps or noise-canceling headphones.

8. Get **Enough Sleep**: Getting enough sleep is essential for maintaining focus and productivity. Make sure to prioritize sleep and establish a consistent sleep routine.

9. **Stay Organized**: Being organized can help you focus on what's important. Keep your workspace clean and tidy, and make sure to prioritize your tasks.

10. **Practice Single-Tasking**: Multitasking can be a distraction and reduce your ability to focus. Instead, try to focus on one task at a time and complete it before moving on to the next one.

Improving your focus requires practice and dedication. By adopting these ten habits, you can improve your ability to concentrate and become a more productive entrepreneur.

Optimism

Optimism can be defined as a general attitude of hope and confidence about the future. In the context of entrepreneurship, it refers to the ability to maintain a positive outlook even in the face of uncertainty and risk. Optimistic entrepreneurs believe they can succeed despite the odds and are willing to take calculated risks to achieve their goals.

Optimism is important for aspiring entrepreneurs for several reasons. Firstly, it provides the motivation and resilience needed to face the inevitable challenges and setbacks that come with starting and growing a business. An optimistic mindset helps entrepreneurs maintain a positive outlook and a can-do attitude in the face of adversity. This can be critical to their ability to persevere and overcome obstacles.

Secondly, optimism can be contagious. As entrepreneurs work to build and promote their businesses, their positive attitudes can inspire others, including potential investors, customers, and employees. This can help create a positive company culture and attract the resources needed to support the venture.

Thirdly, optimism can help entrepreneurs identify and pursue opportunities. By maintaining a positive outlook and a willingness to take risks, entrepreneurs are more likely to see opportunities where others see only challenges or obstacles. They are also more likely to take action to pursue these opportunities, even if they involve a degree of uncertainty or risk.

In short, optimism is an important characteristic for aspiring entrepreneurs to possess. It provides the motivation, resilience, and positive attitude needed to face challenges, inspire others, and identify and pursue opportunities. Entrepreneurs who maintain an optimistic outlook are more likely to achieve success in their ventures than those who do not.

LEARNING TO BE AN OPTIMIST

Optimism can certainly be learned, according to Martin Seligman, the author of *Learned Optimism*. Let's highlight the principles and takeaways that he suggests for learning to be more optimistic.

Learned Optimism, provides a roadmap for individuals to become more optimistic. The book argues that optimism is not a trait that people are born with, but rather a skill that can be learned through practice and training. Here are some principles and takeaways from the book:

1. **Recognize the Three Ps**: According to Seligman, individuals who are optimistic tend to explain negative events as temporary, specific, and external, rather than permanent, pervasive, and personal. These are known as the "three Ps" - personalization, pervasiveness, and permanence. Optimists tend to see negative events as isolated incidents that don't reflect their overall abilities or character.

2. **Practice Cognitive Restructuring**: Cognitive restructuring is a technique that involves replacing negative thoughts with positive ones. For example, instead of saying "I'm not good at this," an optimist might say, "I can get better at this with practice." By changing the way you think about events, you can become more optimistic.

3. **Develop a Growth Mindset**: Optimists tend to have a growth mindset, which means they believe their abilities can improve with effort and practice. You can become more optimistic about your abilities and potential by adopting a growth mindset.

4. **Practice Gratitude**: Gratitude is a key component of optimism. You can cultivate a more positive outlook by focusing on the good things in your life and expressing gratitude for them.

5. **Build Resilience**: Resilience is the ability to bounce back from setbacks and challenges. You can become more optimistic and see setbacks as temporary and surmountable by building resilience.

6. **Surround Yourself with Positive People**: Optimism is contagious, so surrounding yourself with positive, optimistic people can help you cultivate a more positive outlook.

7. **Practice Mindfulness**: Mindfulness involves paying attention to the present moment without judgment. You can develop a more positive relationship with your thoughts and emotions by practicing mindfulness.

Overall, Seligman's book suggests that optimism is a skill that can be learned through intentional effort and practice. By adopting these principles and techniques, individuals can become more optimistic and develop an entrepreneurial mindset characterized by a belief in their own abilities and a positive outlook on the future.

HOW SQUARESPACE FOUNDER AND CEO ANTHONY CASALENA HAS EXHIBITED AN ENTREPRENEURIAL MINDSET

Anthony Casalena is the founder and CEO of Squarespace, a leading website-building and hosting platform. With over two million subscribers and 1,200 employees, Squarespace is recognized as a company led by a CEO with a strong entrepreneurial mindset.

From the very beginning, Casalena exhibited a high need for achievement. As a computer science student at the University of Maryland, he was designing and selling websites to clients. Dissatisfied with the existing website-building platforms, he decided to develop his own. In 2003, while still in college, he launched Squarespace as a part-time venture. Upon graduating in 2005, Casalena believed in the potential of his business and worked on Squarespace full-time.

Casalena's individualism is reflected in his approach to running Squarespace. He has maintained complete control of the company by bootstrapping it with his own savings and avoiding outside funding until 2010. Even after raising over $290 million in venture funding, he has maintained a strong focus on his vision and values for the company.

As the CEO of Squarespace, Casalena exhibits a strong internal locus of control. He has made all major decisions for the company and has been integrally involved in the product development process. This approach has enabled him to maintain a clear vision for the company and to be flexible and adaptable in the face of challenges.

Casalena's focus is evident in his attention to detail and the user experience. He has built Squarespace with a focus on design, which has resulted in a beautiful and intuitive platform that is easy to use for customers with varying levels of technical expertise. His focus on creating a superior user experience has been a major factor in the success of Squarespace.

Casalena is an optimist. He has a positive outlook on the future of Squarespace and is not deterred by setbacks. When Squarespace's first product launch failed, Casalena focused on improving and relaunching it.

Today, Squarespace is recognized as a leading website building and hosting platform, with millions of subscribers around the world.

In conclusion, Anthony Casalena's entrepreneurial mindset has been instrumental in the success of Squarespace. His high need for achievement, individualism, internal locus of control, focus, and optimism have enabled him to build a company admired for its design, user experience, and innovative products. His dedication to his vision and values, and his willingness to take risks and persevere in the face of challenges, have made Squarespace a leading company in the website building and hosting industry.

84

7. Entrepreneurial Motivation

The biggest risk is not taking any risk.
In a world that is changing quickly,
the only strategy that is guaranteed to fail is not taking risks.

Mark Zuckerberg
Co-founder and CEO of Facebook

Entrepreneurial motivation encompasses the factors that initiate, energize, and maintain goal-directed behavior. For entrepreneurial strategic decision-making, three factors are emphasized: *self-efficacy, cognitive motivation,* and *tolerance for ambiguity.*

The Opportunity Analysis Canvas

Emphasis on "Entrepreneurial Motivation"

Entrepreneurial Motivation
Self-efficacy
Cognitive motivation
Tolerance for ambiguity

Entrepreneurial Mindset

Entrepreneurial Behavior

Motivation is critical to the success of entrepreneurship. Starting and sustaining a business through tough times requires a strong sense of purpose and drive. Entrepreneurs need to be intrinsically motivated to overcome the numerous challenges of starting and growing a business.

Motivation drives entrepreneurs to take action, whether creating a new product, developing a marketing strategy, or hiring employees. Without motivation, entrepreneurs may lack the necessary energy and determination to move forward and accomplish their goals.

In addition, motivation can help entrepreneurs overcome obstacles and setbacks. Starting a business involves a significant amount of uncertainty and risk, and it's common for entrepreneurs to face setbacks and failures. A high level of motivation can help entrepreneurs bounce back from these challenges and continue moving forward with resilience and determination.

Moreover, motivation is critical in shaping an entrepreneur's mindset. The entrepreneurial journey is long and challenging, and entrepreneurs must maintain their focus and determination over an extended period. A strong sense of motivation can help entrepreneurs remain persistent and committed to their goals. It can also help them be creative and adaptable when encountering unexpected challenges.

Ultimately, motivation is key to achieving success in entrepreneurship. It drives entrepreneurs to pursue their vision, take calculated risks, and persevere through adversity. The most successful entrepreneurs are highly motivated, passionate, and driven to make their dreams a reality.

KEY FACTORS OF ENTREPRENEURIAL MOTIVATION

Entrepreneurial motivation is a crucial factor that drives an individual towards entrepreneurial activities. Three factors of entrepreneurial motivation are self-efficacy, cognitive motivation, and tolerance for ambiguity.

1. Self-efficacy refers to an individual's belief in their capability to complete a specific task or achieve a specific goal. This belief in oneself plays a vital role in entrepreneurial success. In the context of entrepreneurship, self-efficacy refers to an individual's belief in their capability to start and run a business successfully. It is important for entrepreneurs to have high self-efficacy because it affects their confidence in making decisions, setting goals, and taking risks. High self-efficacy is associated with a greater willingness to take risks, which is a critical aspect of entrepreneurship.

2. Cognitive motivation refers to an individual's internal drive to engage in a specific activity, which is not necessarily driven by external rewards. In the context of entrepreneurship, cognitive motivation is important because it drives an individual to pursue their entrepreneurial goals. It is a self-directed force that encourages entrepreneurs to take initiative, persist in the face of adversity, and innovate. It is driven by the desire to make a meaningful impact on the world through one's business. Entrepreneurs with high levels of cognitive motivation are more likely to persist in the face of challenges and be successful in their ventures.

3. Tolerance for ambiguity is an individual's ability to deal with uncertainty and ambiguity in a given situation. In the context of entrepreneurship, ambiguity is a common experience. It is important for entrepreneurs to have a high tolerance for ambiguity as it allows them to deal with unexpected changes and challenges that arise in their business. A high tolerance for ambiguity enables

entrepreneurs to be flexible, adaptable, and responsive to changing circumstances. It also allows them to see opportunities where others might see only uncertainty.

These factors of entrepreneurial motivation work in conjunction to drive an individual towards entrepreneurial activities. Entrepreneurs with high levels of self-efficacy, cognitive motivation, and tolerance for ambiguity are more likely to succeed in their ventures. They have the confidence to pursue their entrepreneurial goals, the internal drive to innovate and create, and the ability to deal with ambiguity and uncertainty.

Self-efficacy

Self-efficacy refers to an individual's belief in their ability to perform a specific task or achieve a particular goal. Aspiring entrepreneurs with high self-efficacy are more likely to take calculated risks and persist in the face of setbacks and challenges. They are confident in their ability to acquire the necessary skills, knowledge, and resources to launch and grow a successful venture. Conversely, entrepreneurs with low self-efficacy may feel overwhelmed and doubt their ability to start and run a successful business, leading them to avoid or give up on entrepreneurship altogether.

Research has shown that self-efficacy is positively associated with entrepreneurial success. A study conducted by the Global Entrepreneurship Monitor found that entrepreneurs with high self-efficacy were more likely to start and grow successful businesses. Additionally, a study conducted by the University of Iowa found that entrepreneurs with higher levels of self-efficacy were more likely to seek and obtain funding from venture capitalists.

It is important for aspiring entrepreneurs to recognize and develop their self-efficacy beliefs. By taking on new challenges and seeking opportunities to develop their skills and knowledge, they can increase their confidence in their ability to start and run a successful venture. They can also seek out mentors and role models who can provide guidance and support and cultivate a strong social network of other entrepreneurs who can offer advice, share experiences, and provide support.

In summary, self-efficacy is a critical factor in entrepreneurial motivation that can significantly impact an individual's decision to pursue entrepreneurship and their success in doing so. Aspiring entrepreneurs should focus on developing their self-efficacy beliefs to increase their confidence and resilience in pursuing their business goals.

THE ROLE OF EXPERIENCES, FEEDBACK, AND MODELING IN SELF-EFFICACY

Past experiences, feedback, and modeling play an essential role in developing and strengthening an entrepreneur's self-efficacy. Past experiences, both successes and failures, can have a significant impact on an individual's confidence in their ability to perform specific tasks. Successful experiences can boost self-efficacy, while failed attempts can diminish it. An entrepreneur who has experienced success in launching a previous venture may have high self-efficacy in starting a new one. On the other hand, an individual who has experienced significant setbacks may struggle with self-doubt and have low self-efficacy in pursuing a new venture.

Feedback from others can also play a role in shaping an entrepreneur's self-efficacy. Positive feedback can increase confidence, while negative feedback can have the opposite effect. As such, it is crucial for entrepreneurs to surround themselves with individuals who are supportive and provide constructive feedback. Being around individuals who are negative and unsupportive can lead to decreased self-efficacy.

Modeling refers to the observation of others performing a specific task. An entrepreneur may develop self-efficacy through observing others who have successfully achieved a similar goal. Observing the success of others can lead an individual to believe that they, too, can achieve the same level of success. It is important to note that the effectiveness of modeling can depend on the perceived similarity between the observer and the model. For example, an entrepreneur who observes someone from a similar background achieving success may be more likely to develop self-efficacy than someone who observes a successful individual from a different background.

In summary, past experiences, feedback, and modeling can significantly impact an entrepreneur's self-efficacy. Positive experiences, constructive feedback, and effective models can lead to increased self-efficacy, while negative experiences, negative feedback, and poor models can lead to decreased self-efficacy. Aspiring entrepreneurs can benefit from reflecting on their past experiences, seeking out supportive feedback, and identifying effective models to help build and maintain their self-efficacy.

TECHNIQUES FOR BUILDING SELF-EFFICACY

Building self-efficacy is a critical aspect of developing an entrepreneurial mindset. The following techniques can be used to improve self-efficacy:

1. **Mastery Experiences**: Successful experiences can be instrumental in building self-efficacy. By setting and achieving small goals, entrepreneurs can create a sense of accomplishment that contributes to their belief in their ability to achieve future goals. Mastery experiences not only enhance an entrepreneur's confidence in their skills and abilities but also help develop a positive self-image.

2. **Social Persuasion**: Entrepreneurs who receive encouragement from others are more likely to believe in their own abilities. By receiving positive feedback and support from others, entrepreneurs can develop a stronger belief in their ability to succeed. This can be achieved through a mentor, supportive team members, or positive feedback from customers.

3. **Vicarious Experiences**: Observing others succeed in similar situations can help to improve an entrepreneur's self-efficacy. This is particularly important for novice entrepreneurs who have limited experience in the business world. By observing the success of others, entrepreneurs can develop a sense of confidence in their own abilities.

4. **Emotional and Physiological States**: Emotional and physiological states can influence an entrepreneur's self-efficacy. Anxiety and stress can undermine an entrepreneur's belief in their ability to succeed. Entrepreneurs can maintain a positive mindset and build self-efficacy by managing emotional and physiological states. This can be achieved through meditation, physical exercise, or other stress-reducing techniques.

Entrepreneurs who can develop a high level of self-efficacy are more likely to pursue challenging goals and persist in the face of obstacles. This belief in their own ability to succeed can help entrepreneurs overcome setbacks and continue working towards their goals. The techniques listed above can help entrepreneurs to build self-efficacy and achieve success in their ventures.

Cognitive Motivation

Cognitive motivation is the underlying thought processes and mental states that drive individuals towards entrepreneurial action. It involves the beliefs, attitudes, and values entrepreneurs hold about themselves, their ventures, and their environment. Cognitive motivation plays a crucial role in shaping an entrepreneur's decision-making process, risk-taking behavior, and overall success.

Aspiring entrepreneurs who possess a strong cognitive motivation are more likely to identify opportunities and pursue them with a clear vision and conviction. Such individuals possess a set of positive attitudes and values that drive them towards entrepreneurial action, such as a desire for autonomy and creativity, a willingness to take risks, and a belief in their own abilities to succeed. These attitudes enable entrepreneurs to maintain a positive mindset even when faced with challenges and setbacks, allowing them to persist and adapt in adverse times.

On the other hand, entrepreneurs with a weak cognitive motivation may struggle to overcome obstacles and setbacks. They may lack confidence and belief in their own abilities, leading them to avoid risk and miss opportunities. As a result, they may be less likely to achieve success in their ventures.

Therefore, it is crucial for aspiring entrepreneurs to cultivate a strong cognitive motivation. This can be achieved through introspection, education, and practice. Entrepreneurs can identify their own values, attitudes, and beliefs and work to reinforce and develop those that support their entrepreneurial goals. They can seek out education and training to develop skills and knowledge that enhance their confidence and ability to pursue opportunities. They can also practice positive self-talk, visualization, and other cognitive techniques that help maintain a positive mindset and reinforce their beliefs in their own abilities.

Aspiring entrepreneurs can increase their chances of success in their ventures by developing strong cognitive motivation. They will be better equipped to identify and pursue opportunities, take calculated risks, and overcome challenges and setbacks along the way.

THE ROLE OF GOALS AND GOAL ORIENTATION IN COGNITIVE MOTIVATION

Goals are a central component of cognitive motivation in entrepreneurship. They provide a sense of direction and purpose, helping entrepreneurs to focus their energy and resources. Additionally, goals help entrepreneurs establish progress benchmarks and measure their success. A key aspect of goals is the level of goal orientation, which refers to the degree to which an entrepreneur is motivated by the pursuit of specific goals.

There are two main types of goal orientation: task orientation and ego orientation. Task orientation is characterized by a focus on the learning process and personal improvement with an emphasis on developing new skills and achieving mastery. On the other hand, ego orientation is characterized by a focus on demonstrating ability and proving oneself to others emphasizing winning and achieving recognition.

For aspiring entrepreneurs, developing a strong task orientation to support their cognitive motivation is important. By focusing on the learning process and personal growth, entrepreneurs can better adapt to new challenges and opportunities while also developing a strong sense of resilience and persistence. By contrast, ego orientation can lead to a narrow focus on short-term gains and a lack of flexibility.

In addition to goal orientation, it is important for entrepreneurs to set specific, challenging goals that are aligned with their personal values and long-term aspirations. By setting clear and meaningful goals, entrepreneurs can stay motivated and engaged in pursuing their ventures. Moreover, setting and achieving goals can help entrepreneurs develop a sense of self-efficacy as they build confidence in their ability to execute their plans and achieve their objectives.

Finally, goal setting and attainment can also foster a sense of autonomy and control for entrepreneurs. By setting goals and working towards them on their own terms, entrepreneurs can take ownership of their ventures and develop a strong sense of personal agency. This can be a powerful motivator, driving entrepreneurs to take bold action and pursue their entrepreneurial ambitions with passion and determination.

TECHNIQUES FOR ENHANCING COGNITIVE MOTIVATION

Entrepreneurial success depends on several factors, including motivation. Cognitive motivation is an essential component of an entrepreneurial mindset and involves setting challenging goals and the desire to achieve them. Techniques for enhancing cognitive motivation are essential for entrepreneurs to achieve their goals and stay motivated. Here are three techniques that can help entrepreneurs enhance cognitive motivation:

- **Setting Specific, Challenging Goals**: Entrepreneurs must set specific and challenging goals to achieve success. By setting goals, entrepreneurs can focus on what they want to achieve and develop a clear path to reach those goals. Goals should be specific, measurable, and have a timeline for achievement. Specific, challenging goals give entrepreneurs a clear understanding of what they need to do to succeed and can enhance their motivation to achieve them.

- **Adopting a Growth Mindset**: A growth mindset is essential for entrepreneurs who want to enhance their cognitive motivation. This mindset involves believing they can develop their skills and abilities through hard work and dedication. By adopting a growth mindset, entrepreneurs can learn from their mistakes and failures and use them as opportunities for growth and improvement.

- **Developing a Sense of Purpose**: A sense of purpose is crucial for entrepreneurs who want to enhance their cognitive motivation. A sense of purpose involves clearly understanding why they are doing what they are doing. Entrepreneurs with a sense of purpose are more likely to stay motivated and committed to achieving their goals in times of prosperity as well as peril.

In conclusion, cognitive motivation is an essential component of an entrepreneurial mindset. By setting specific, challenging goals, adopting a growth mindset, and developing a sense of purpose, entrepreneurs can enhance their cognitive motivation and achieve their goals. These techniques can help entrepreneurs stay motivated, even when they face challenges and setbacks, and increase their chances of success.

Tolerance for Ambiguity

Tolerance for ambiguity is the ability to function effectively in situations without clear and certain knowledge of what is happening or what will happen. In entrepreneurship, ambiguity is often present because of the risks, uncertainties, and unpredictability of starting and running a business. Therefore, entrepreneurs with a high level of tolerance for ambiguity are better equipped to deal with the challenges and setbacks they face and adapt to changing circumstances.

Tolerance for ambiguity is particularly important for aspiring entrepreneurs because they are likely to encounter a variety of ambiguous situations in their entrepreneurial journey. They may face uncertain market conditions, changing customer preferences, unpredictable technological advancements, and unexpected financial challenges. Being able to handle such ambiguity can help them make sound decisions, take calculated risks, and remain focused on their goals.

Entrepreneurs who have a high level of tolerance for ambiguity are more likely to thrive in environments of uncertainty, where new ideas and opportunities are often found. They are more likely to view challenges as opportunities for learning and growth instead of insurmountable barriers. They are also more likely to experiment and take risks, as they are less deterred by the potential negative consequences of failure.

Moreover, in today's rapidly changing business environment, tolerance for ambiguity has become an increasingly important trait for entrepreneurs. As technological advancements continue to disrupt traditional industries and create new markets, entrepreneurs need to be able to navigate ambiguity and adapt to changes quickly. By having a high level of tolerance for ambiguity, entrepreneurs can remain agile and innovative, seizing opportunities as they arise.

In summary, tolerance for ambiguity is a critical trait for entrepreneurs, as it allows them to navigate uncertain and unpredictable situations, take calculated risks, and adapt to changes in the business environment. Entrepreneurs who possess a high level of tolerance for ambiguity are more likely to be successful in their ventures, as they can remain focused on their goals, take advantage of opportunities, and learn from their experiences.

THE ROLE OF RISK AND UNCERTAINTY IN ENTREPRENEURSHIP.

Risk and uncertainty are two major elements of entrepreneurship. While risk is an inherent feature of any business venture, uncertainty can arise from various sources like market changes, technological developments, regulatory environments, and unexpected events. Both risk and uncertainty can lead to potential rewards, but they also pose a significant challenge to entrepreneurs.

Entrepreneurs are often required to make decisions in an environment of ambiguity, where they have limited information and must navigate unknown or unpredictable situations. The ability to tolerate ambiguity involves being comfortable with the unknown and having the capacity to deal with uncertain situations.

To successfully manage risk and uncertainty, entrepreneurs must be willing to take calculated risks and make decisions in the face of incomplete or conflicting information. They must be willing to tolerate ambiguity, recognize that not all risks can be eliminated, and be willing to learn from failure. Entrepreneurs who can tolerate ambiguity are more likely to be innovative, creative, and adapt quickly to changing market conditions.

Tolerance for ambiguity also requires embracing the unknown and being comfortable with change. This can be difficult for some individuals who prefer a structured and predictable environment. However, entrepreneurs who are able to tolerate ambiguity can recognize opportunities that others may miss and can take action quickly to capitalize on them. They are able to develop creative solutions to complex problems and are not afraid to take risks.

In summary, tolerance for ambiguity is an important attribute for entrepreneurs. It allows them to navigate a business environment's risks and uncertainties and take calculated risks to achieve their goals. By being comfortable with the unknown, entrepreneurs can recognize opportunities others may miss and develop creative solutions to complex problems.

TECHNIQUES FOR BUILDING TOLERANCE FOR AMBIGUITY

Building tolerance for ambiguity is an important aspect of entrepreneurial motivation that can be developed through various techniques. Here are four key techniques that can help aspiring entrepreneurs build their tolerance for ambiguity:

1. **Exposure to Uncertainty**: One of the most effective ways to build tolerance for ambiguity is to actively seek out experiences that involve uncertainty. This could include taking on new challenges, traveling to unfamiliar places, or engaging in new activities. By exposing yourself to situations that are outside of your comfort zone, you can gradually become more comfortable with ambiguity and uncertainty.

2. **Reframing**: Another way to build tolerance for ambiguity is to reframe the way you think about uncertain situations. Rather than seeing ambiguity as a threat, try to see it as an opportunity for growth and learning. By reframing uncertainty in this way, you can develop a more positive attitude toward it and become more comfortable with it over time.

3. **Seeking Diverse Perspectives**: Exposing yourself to diverse perspectives can also help build your tolerance for ambiguity. This could involve seeking out feedback from people with different backgrounds and experiences or working with team members who have different skill sets and ways of thinking. By embracing diversity, you can learn to appreciate different viewpoints and become more comfortable with ambiguity.

4. **Embracing Failure**: Finally, embracing failure is an essential part of building tolerance for ambiguity. Rather than seeing failure as a negative outcome, try to see it as a learning opportunity. By learning from your mistakes and failures, you can become more comfortable with uncertainty and develop a more positive attitude toward it.

In summary, building tolerance for ambiguity is an important aspect of entrepreneurial motivation that can be developed through exposure to uncertainty, reframing, seeking out diverse perspectives, and embracing failure. By actively working to build your tolerance for ambiguity, you can become a more confident and effective entrepreneur who is better equipped to handle the challenges and uncertainties of starting and growing a business.

Case Studies of Motivated Entrepreneurs

Sara Blakely

Sara Blakely is a prime example of someone who embodies the entrepreneurial mindset and motivation required for success. She is the founder of Spanx, a women's undergarment company that revolutionized the shapewear industry. She was born and raised in Clearwater, Florida, and had no prior experience in the fashion industry before launching her company.

Blakely's self-efficacy was critical in launching Spanx. She was confident in her ability to start a business and sell her product, despite having no prior experience. Her belief in herself and her product was so strong that she spent two years developing it before even trying to sell it. Her self-efficacy was further bolstered by feedback from her friends and family, who were enthusiastic about the product.

Cognitive motivation was also a key factor in Blakely's success. She set specific, challenging goals for herself and her company. In fact, her first goal was to get her product on Oprah's Favorite Things list, which she achieved just one year after launching Spanx. She also developed a growth mindset, always looking for ways to improve and learn from her experiences.

Blakely's tolerance for ambiguity was critical in overcoming her challenges as a new entrepreneur. She was willing to take risks and embrace failure. One of her most significant challenges was finding a manufacturer to produce her product. After being turned down by countless manufacturers, she finally found one in North Carolina that was willing to partner with her for production. However, when the first shipment arrived, she realized that the dye lot was off, and the product was a beige color that was unappealing to customers. Instead of giving up, Blakely decided to embrace the mistake and sell the product as "nude." It became a popular color and is still one of the company's best sellers.

In summary, Sara Blakely's success as an entrepreneur can be attributed to her strong entrepreneurial motivation. She had a high level of self-efficacy, set challenging goals, and had a growth mindset. She was also willing to take risks and embrace failure, which allowed her to overcome the challenges she faced as a new entrepreneur. Her story is an inspiration for aspiring entrepreneurs who may be facing similar challenges in their own ventures.

Lisa Price

Lisa Price, the founder of Carol's Daughter, is a prime example of how entrepreneurial motivation can drive success. Carol's Daughter is a beauty and haircare brand that creates natural products that celebrate black women's beauty.

Lisa's story began in 1992, when she was working a full-time job at a TV studio and spent her free time crafting natural beauty products in her kitchen. The idea for Carol's Daughter came when her mother suggested that she sell her products at a church flea market. This led to Price opening a store in Brooklyn, New York, where she sold her products.

However, the journey was not easy, and Lisa faced several setbacks, including financial struggles and losing her store in a fire. Despite this, she never gave up, and her persistence and determination kept her going. She took the opportunity to sell her products online and eventually moved into retail stores, including Sephora and Macy's.

Lisa's entrepreneurial motivation played a vital role in her success. She had a clear vision for her brand and was motivated to create products that catered to Black women's beauty needs. Her passion for natural beauty products and desire to cater to an underserved market motivated her to keep pushing forward despite challenges.

Lisa's self-efficacy was evident in the way she taught herself how to create beauty products and build a successful business. She used customer feedback to improve her products and build a loyal following. Her ability to set specific goals and track her progress was crucial in building her business, and her focus on her purpose kept her motivated.

Tolerance for ambiguity was also essential for Lisa's success. The natural beauty industry was new and relatively unknown at the time, and Lisa had to navigate the uncertainty and take risks. She sought diverse perspectives to better understand the industry and embraced failures as an opportunity to learn and grow.

In conclusion, Lisa Price's success with Carol's Daughter is a testament to the importance of entrepreneurial motivation. Her self-efficacy, cognitive motivation, and tolerance for ambiguity drove her to turn her passion into a successful business. Her story is an inspiration to aspiring entrepreneurs to never give up on their dreams and to use their motivation to overcome any challenges they may face.

Cathy Hughes

Cathy Hughes is an American entrepreneur and media executive who founded the media company Urban One, which has become the largest African American-owned broadcasting company in the United States. Hughes' story is an inspiring example of how strong motivation and determination can help entrepreneurs overcome challenges and achieve remarkable success.

Cathy Hughes was born in Omaha, Nebraska, in 1947. She grew up in a family of modest means and faced numerous challenges, including poverty, racism, and health problems. Despite these challenges, Hughes was determined to succeed and worked hard to achieve her goals.

In the late 1970s, Hughes moved to Washington, D.C., and began working in the radio industry. She quickly rose through the ranks and became a popular on-air personality. However, Hughes soon realized there were few opportunities for African Americans in the radio industry and decided to start her own business.

In 1980, Hughes founded Radio One, a broadcasting company focused on serving African American audiences. The company's first station, WOL, quickly became a success, and Hughes used the profits to acquire additional stations. In 1999, the company went public, and Hughes became the first African American woman to head a publicly traded company.

Hughes faced numerous challenges along the way, including discrimination, financial difficulties, and health problems. However, she was motivated by her desire to create opportunities for African Americans and provide high-quality programming that reflected their experiences and interests.

Hughes is known for her strong work ethic and ability to motivate and inspire her employees. She has said that her success is due to her ability to focus on her goals, maintain a positive attitude, and persevere in the face of obstacles.

Today, Urban One is a thriving media company with radio stations, television networks, and digital media platforms. Hughes continues to play an active role in the company and is recognized as a trailblazer and a role model for aspiring entrepreneurs. Her story is a powerful example of how entrepreneurial motivation can help individuals overcome challenges and achieve their goals.

Summary

Self-efficacy, cognitive motivation, and tolerance for ambiguity are three critical factors that affect entrepreneurial motivation.

Self-efficacy is an individual's belief in their ability to perform a specific task successfully or achieve a specific goal. It is essential for entrepreneurs to have high self-efficacy, as this belief in their abilities can help them overcome obstacles, take calculated risks, and persist through failures. By leveraging techniques such as mastery experiences, social persuasion, vicarious experiences, and emotional and physiological states, entrepreneurs can build their self-efficacy and increase their chances of success.

Cognitive motivation refers to the mental processes that drive an individual's behavior towards achieving their goals. Cognitive motivation is crucial for entrepreneurs. By leveraging techniques such as setting specific, challenging goals, adopting a growth mindset, and developing a sense of purpose, entrepreneurs can enhance their cognitive motivation and keep themselves focused on their objectives.

Tolerance for ambiguity refers to an individual's ability to handle uncertain, unfamiliar, or changing situations. Entrepreneurs must have a high level of tolerance for ambiguity because starting a business is inherently risky and often involves navigating unfamiliar and uncertain situations. By building tolerance for ambiguity through exposure to uncertainty, reframing, seeking out diverse perspectives, and embracing failure, entrepreneurs can handle the uncertainty and ambiguity of entrepreneurship more effectively.

Entrepreneurs with high levels of self-efficacy, cognitive motivation, and tolerance for ambiguity are better equipped to handle the challenges of starting and growing a business. By utilizing the techniques discussed above, entrepreneurs can develop these traits and increase their chances of success.

8. Entrepreneurial Behavior

Surround yourself only with people who are going to lift you higher.

Oprah Winfrey

Media proprietor, actress, producer, and philanthropist

Entrepreneurial mindset and motivation can only translate into action if *entrepreneurial behaviors* exist. While there are many behaviors that may be described as entrepreneurial, we'll focus on the four behaviors most critical to entrepreneurial opportunity analysis and action: *confidence, risk, interpersonal skills,* and *social capital.*

The Opportunity Analysis Canvas

Emphasis on "Entrepreneurial Behavior"

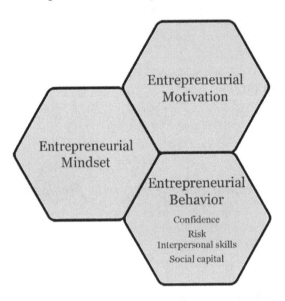

Entrepreneurial behaviors play a critical role in translating mindset and motivation into action. Entrepreneurial mindset and motivation are important for generating ideas and identifying opportunities, but they need to be coupled with the right behaviors to achieve success.

Confidence is a critical entrepreneurial behavior. Successful entrepreneurs often have high levels of self-confidence that allow them to take risks and pursue their goals with conviction. This confidence also helps them navigate challenges and setbacks, which are inevitable in any entrepreneurial journey. Without confidence, entrepreneurs may be hesitant to act, which can impede their progress and ultimately lead to failure.

Risk-taking is another important behavior for entrepreneurs. Entrepreneurship is inherently risky, as it involves pursuing untested ideas and venturing into unknown territory. Successful entrepreneurs are often willing to take calculated risks in order to achieve their goals. This doesn't mean that they are reckless or take unnecessary risks, but rather that they are comfortable with uncertainty and are able to assess the potential benefits and drawbacks of a given opportunity.

Interpersonal skills are also critical for entrepreneurs. Entrepreneurs need must communicate effectively with others in order to build relationships, pitch their ideas, and collaborate with partners and stakeholders. Strong interpersonal skills can also help entrepreneurs identify and address customer needs and manage employees and other team members effectively.

Social capital is also an important entrepreneurial behavior. Social capital refers to the network of relationships that entrepreneurs build over time. These relationships can include mentors, advisors, investors, and other stakeholders who provide support, guidance, and resources to help entrepreneurs achieve their goals. Building strong social capital is critical for success in entrepreneurship, as it can help entrepreneurs to access new opportunities, expand their knowledge and expertise, and build a strong reputation in their industry.

In conclusion, while entrepreneurial mindset and motivation are important for generating ideas and identifying opportunities, these factors alone are not enough to achieve entrepreneurial success. The right entrepreneurial behaviors are critical for translating mindset and motivation into action, and for navigating the challenges and uncertainties that come with starting and growing a business.

Confidence

Confidence in the context of entrepreneurship refers to the belief in oneself and one's abilities to succeed in a given entrepreneurial venture. It is the degree to which an entrepreneur believes that they possess the necessary skills, knowledge, and experience to overcome obstacles and achieve their goals. Confidence is a key factor in entrepreneurial success, as it enables entrepreneurs to take risks and make decisions in the face of uncertainty.

Confidence is closely linked to self-efficacy, which is the belief in one's ability to successfully perform specific tasks or achieve specific goals. A high level of self-efficacy can lead to greater confidence, as it provides a foundation for the belief that one can achieve success in a given area.

Confidence can also be influenced by past experiences, feedback from others, and the level of social support an entrepreneur receives. A history of success in past entrepreneurial ventures can boost an entrepreneur's confidence, while negative feedback or lack of support can undermine it.

In the entrepreneurial context, confidence is a personal trait and an important business asset. Entrepreneurs who project confidence are more likely to attract investors, partners, and customers because confidence can signal competence, credibility, and conviction in their vision. Confidence can also be contagious, inspiring team members and others to share in the entrepreneur's vision and commitment to success.

THE ROLE OF SELF-EFFICACY IN BUILDING CONFIDENCE FOR ENTREPRENEURS

Self-efficacy plays a critical role in building confidence for entrepreneurs. Self-efficacy is an individual's belief in their ability to perform a specific task or achieve a certain goal. Regarding entrepreneurship, having high levels of self-efficacy can lead to higher levels of confidence, which is an important factor in taking action and making decisions.

Entrepreneurship is a challenging and uncertain path, and entrepreneurs face many obstacles and setbacks along the way. However, those with high levels of self-efficacy tend to view these challenges as opportunities for growth, rather than insurmountable obstacles. They believe in their ability to overcome these challenges and solve problems.

In contrast, individuals with low self-efficacy may struggle to build confidence in their abilities as entrepreneurs. They may doubt their ability to make good decisions, overcome obstacles, or take risks, leading to hesitation or even inaction.

Entrepreneurs can build their self-efficacy and, as a result, their confidence, through a variety of techniques, such as setting and achieving small goals, seeking feedback and mentorship, and using positive self-talk.

TECHNIQUES FOR BUILDING CONFIDENCE

Building and maintaining confidence is a critical component of entrepreneurial success. While some people seem naturally confident, others may need to work on developing and maintaining their confidence.

Here are four techniques for building confidence:

- **Positive Self-talk**: Self-talk is the internal dialogue you have with yourself, and it can significantly impact your confidence. If you find yourself thinking negative thoughts, such as "I'm not good enough," or "I can't do this," try replacing them with positive affirmations, such as "I am capable and competent," or "I can handle any challenge that comes my way." By repeating positive affirmations, you can reprogram your mind to believe in your abilities.

- **Visualization**: Visualization is the practice of imagining yourself succeeding in a particular situation. By visualizing yourself achieving your goals, you can increase your confidence and reduce anxiety. To use this technique, try picturing yourself giving a successful pitch or closing a big deal. By seeing yourself succeeding, you can increase your chances of success.

- **Seeking Feedback**: Seeking feedback from others can be a powerful way to build confidence. By getting input from others, you can learn about your strengths and weaknesses and gain a better understanding of how others perceive you. If you're feeling unsure about your abilities, try asking for feedback from a trusted friend, mentor, or colleague. By hearing positive feedback and constructive criticism, you can build confidence and improve your skills.

- **Taking Action**: Taking action is one of the best ways to build confidence. You can prove to yourself that you are capable of success by setting small goals and taking steps toward achieving them. If you're feeling unsure of yourself, try setting a small goal and taking action to achieve it. As you achieve small successes, your confidence will grow, and you'll be more likely to take on bigger challenges in the future.

ENTREPRENEURS WHO EXHIBITED CONFIDENCE IN THEIR ACTIONS

There are many entrepreneurs who have exhibited confidence in their actions, breaking through barriers to build successful businesses:

- **Katrina Lake:** Lake exhibited confidence in her ability to disrupt the fashion industry. She founded Stitch Fix, an online styling service that uses data and algorithms to curate personalized clothing recommendations for customers. Despite facing doubts from some investors who thought the business model was too risky, Lake remained confident in her idea and took the company public in 2017.
- **Whitney Wolfe Herd:** Whitney Wolfe Herd exhibited confidence in her ability to create a dating app that empowered women. She left Tinder to start her own company, Bumble, which requires women to make the first move when initiating conversations. Despite facing pushback and skepticism from some investors and industry insiders, Herd remained confident in her vision and successfully built Bumble into a billion-dollar business.
- **Rihanna:** Rihanna exhibited confidence in her ability to create a beauty line that was inclusive of all skin tones. She launched Fenty Beauty with a wide range of shades, becoming a trailblazer in the industry. Despite facing criticism and pushback from some beauty companies, Rihanna remained confident in her vision and built a successful brand.

These entrepreneurs all demonstrated confidence in their abilities to disrupt industries and build successful businesses. They faced challenges and obstacles, but remained steadfast in their beliefs and were ultimately successful in their endeavors.

Risk

Risk-taking is a fundamental aspect of entrepreneurship, which involves making decisions and taking actions in the face of uncertainty and potential loss. In the context of entrepreneurship, risk-taking refers to the willingness of an entrepreneur to take calculated and strategic risks in pursuit of their goals and objectives. Risk-taking involves taking actions that have an uncertain outcome, which may result in either success or failure.

Taking risks is essential in entrepreneurship because the environment in which entrepreneurs operate is unpredictable and constantly changing. The entrepreneur must be prepared to take risks to create new products, enter new markets, and develop innovative strategies. However, taking risks does not mean acting recklessly. Instead, it involves careful analysis of the situation and identifying potential risks and rewards.

Risk-taking is an important part of entrepreneurship because it allows entrepreneurs to take advantage of opportunities that would not be possible if they only pursued safe and proven strategies. By taking calculated risks, entrepreneurs can gain a competitive advantage over their competitors and make innovative strides in their respective industries.

Successful entrepreneurs know how to manage risks, and they approach risk-taking in a systematic and methodical way. They gather data and assess the potential outcomes of various options, weigh the pros and cons of each potential action, and make a decision based on their analysis.

In conclusion, risk-taking is an essential element of entrepreneurship that involves taking calculated risks to pursue goals and objectives. While taking risks may be associated with potential losses, successful entrepreneurs know how to manage and mitigate risks while also recognizing the potential rewards.

THE ROLE OF RISK IN CREATING OPPORTUNITIES FOR INNOVATION AND GROWTH

Risk is an inherent component of entrepreneurship that arises from the uncertainty associated with starting a business. Entrepreneurs are willing to take risks to create new products or services, enter new markets, and innovate in their respective industries. Risk-taking is important for entrepreneurs because it enables them to capitalize on opportunities and create value for themselves, their businesses, and their customers.

Innovation and growth are key drivers of risk-taking behavior in entrepreneurship. Innovation involves creating something new or improving upon an existing product or service, while growth is the process of expanding the business by increasing revenues, customers, and market share. Both processes involve risk-taking because entrepreneurs must make strategic decisions about how to allocate resources and invest in new initiatives that have uncertain outcomes.

Risk-taking also allows entrepreneurs to differentiate themselves from their competitors by pursuing opportunities that others may overlook or perceive as too risky. By taking calculated risks, entrepreneurs can gain a competitive advantage and establish themselves as leaders in their respective industries. For example,

Airbnb disrupted the hospitality industry by providing an online platform that allowed individuals to rent out their homes and apartments to travelers. While this business model was seen as risky at first, Airbnb's success in creating a new market and disrupting traditional hospitality chains has made it a household name.

Overall, risk-taking is an essential component of entrepreneurship that enables entrepreneurs to create value, innovate, and differentiate themselves in their respective industries. By taking calculated risks, entrepreneurs can capitalize on opportunities and create long-term growth and success for their businesses.

TYPES OF RISK

Risk is an inherent aspect of entrepreneurship, and entrepreneurs must be able to identify, evaluate, and manage different types of risks to ensure their success. There are four primary types of risks associated with entrepreneurship: financial, reputational, strategic, and psychological.

- **Financial Risk:** This type of risk is related to the financial investments required for starting and growing a business. Entrepreneurs must invest their time, effort, and money into the venture, and there is always a risk that they may not see a return on their investment. Factors such as cash flow, revenue, and profitability can all impact financial risk, and entrepreneurs must be able to manage these variables to minimize risk.

- **Reputational Risk:** This type of risk is related to the potential damage to the entrepreneur's reputation if something goes wrong with the business. Reputational risk can arise from a variety of factors, including poor customer service, low-quality products, or negative media coverage. Entrepreneurs must be able to manage their reputation by delivering high-quality products and services and responding quickly and appropriately to any issues that arise.

- **Strategic Risk**: This type of risk is related to the entrepreneur's ability to develop and implement an effective business strategy. Entrepreneurs must be able to identify opportunities, analyze market trends, and make strategic decisions about the direction of the business. Strategic risk can arise if an entrepreneur makes a poor decision or fails to adapt to changing market conditions.

- **Psychological Risk**: This type of risk is related to the emotional and mental toll of entrepreneurship. Starting and growing a business can be stressful, and as a result, entrepreneurs may experience anxiety, depression, or burnout. Psychological risk can impact an entrepreneur's ability to make sound decisions and manage their business effectively, making it important to prioritize mental health and well-being.

Overall, entrepreneurs must be able to manage these types of risks to ensure the success of their business. By identifying and evaluating potential risks, they can make informed decisions and take steps to minimize risk while maximizing growth and innovation.

TECHNIQUES FOR MANAGING RISK

Managing risk is a crucial aspect of entrepreneurship. Risk management strategies are designed to minimize or mitigate potential losses and maximize opportunities for success. Here are four techniques for managing risk in the entrepreneurial process:

- **Conducting Market Research:** One of the most effective ways to manage risk is to conduct thorough market research before making any significant investments. Market research helps entrepreneurs identify the target market, understand consumer needs, assess the competition, and determine potential demand. This information can help entrepreneurs make informed decisions and reduce the risk of investing in unprofitable ventures.

119

- **Diversifying:** Another way to manage risk is by diversifying investments. Diversification involves spreading investments across different markets, products, or services to reduce the risk of loss. By diversifying, entrepreneurs can avoid putting "all their eggs in one basket" to minimize their risk of loss from exposure to a single market or product.

- **Developing Contingency Plans:** Contingency plans are strategies put in place to manage potential risks and unexpected events. By anticipating potential risks and developing contingency plans, entrepreneurs can minimize the negative impact of unexpected events on their business. Contingency plans may include backup suppliers, alternative marketing strategies, or emergency cash reserves.

- **Seeking Advice from Experts:** Finally, entrepreneurs can reduce risk by seeking advice from experts. By seeking the guidance of experienced professionals, entrepreneurs can learn from their mistakes and avoid potential pitfalls. Experts can provide valuable insights and advice on a wide range of topics, including market trends, financial management, legal issues, and risk management.

In conclusion, risk management is a critical component of the entrepreneurial process. By conducting market research, diversifying investments, developing contingency plans, and seeking advice from experts, entrepreneurs can minimize the risks associated with starting and growing a business. While risk-taking is an essential aspect of entrepreneurship, effective risk management is key to achieving long-term success.

ENTREPRENEURS WHO TOOK CALCULATED RISKS TO SUCCEED

Entrepreneurs have long faced systemic challenges, including limited access to capital and discrimination, which have made starting and growing a business even more difficult. However, many of these entrepreneurs have taken calculated risks and seized opportunities to build successful businesses. Here are a few examples:

- **Madam C.J. Walker** is often considered the first self-made female millionaire in the United States. She started her business selling hair care products for African American women in the early 1900s, and through hard work and perseverance, she built a successful enterprise. She took risks by expanding her business into new markets, developing new products, and investing in marketing and advertising.

- **Reginald F. Lewis** was a lawyer and entrepreneur who is best known for his leveraged buyout of Beatrice International Foods, a multinational food company, in the 1980s. Lewis saw an opportunity to acquire the company and take advantage of its underutilized assets. He took a calculated risk by using a leveraged buyout to finance the acquisition, and he ultimately turned the company around and sold it for a significant profit.

- **Daymond John** is a successful entrepreneur and investor who is best known for his role on the television show Shark Tank. He started his first business, FUBU, in the 1990s, and he took risks by investing his own money in the business and developing new products. He has since gone on to invest in and advise many other successful businesses.

These are just a few examples of entrepreneurs who have taken calculated risks to succeed. Despite the challenges they have faced, these entrepreneurs have demonstrated resilience, perseverance, and a willingness to take risks in pursuit of their goals.

Interpersonal Skills

Interpersonal skills refer to the ability to interact and communicate effectively with others. In the context of entrepreneurship, interpersonal skills are critical to the success of a business as entrepreneurs need to engage with various stakeholders, including customers, employees, suppliers, investors, and other entrepreneurs.

Entrepreneurs with strong interpersonal skills can establish and maintain effective working relationships with these stakeholders, which can lead to increased productivity, collaboration, and innovation. They can effectively communicate their vision, motivate and lead employees, negotiate with suppliers and investors, and build strong networks.

Interpersonal skills include a range of abilities such as active listening, verbal and nonverbal communication, empathy, emotional intelligence, conflict resolution, and networking. Entrepreneurs with strong interpersonal skills can understand the needs and expectations of their stakeholders and communicate with them in a way that builds trust and rapport.

Additionally, entrepreneurs with strong interpersonal skills can better manage conflict and negotiate effectively with suppliers, investors, and other stakeholders. They can also build a strong network of contacts that can provide support, mentorship, and access to resources that can help their business grow.

Overall, strong interpersonal skills are critical for entrepreneurs to build and maintain relationships with their stakeholders and can contribute significantly to the success of their business.

THE IMPORTANCE OF EFFECTIVE COMMUNICATION, NETWORKING, AND RELATIONSHIP-BUILDING FOR ENTREPRENEURS

Effective communication, networking, and relationship-building are critical interpersonal skills that are important for entrepreneurs. These skills allow them to create and maintain relationships with key stakeholders such as customers, suppliers, investors, and employees. The ability to effectively communicate and build relationships can make or break an entrepreneurial venture because relationships are often the key to securing funding, gaining customers, and building a strong team.

Effective communication is essential for entrepreneurs; it enables them to articulate their ideas, goals, and vision clearly to stakeholders. Entrepreneurs must be able to communicate their value proposition to potential customers, explain their business plan to investors, and inspire and motivate their teams. Effective communication skills also help entrepreneurs resolve conflicts and negotiate effectively, which can be critical in maintaining relationships with suppliers and customers.

Networking is also an important interpersonal skill for entrepreneurs; they must be able to identify and engage with potential customers, investors, mentors, and advisors. Networking can help entrepreneurs build a strong support network, gain valuable insights and advice, and identify new opportunities for growth. Networking can also help them establish themselves as thought leaders in their industries, which can help build their brand and reputation.

Relationship-building is another important interpersonal skill for entrepreneurs. Building strong relationships with customers, suppliers, employees, and investors is essential for the long-term success of an entrepreneurial venture. Entrepreneurs must be able to establish trust and credibility with these key stakeholders, which requires the ability to listen and respond to their needs, maintain open lines of communication, and demonstrate a genuine interest in their success.

In summary, effective communication, networking, and relationship-building are essential interpersonal skills for entrepreneurs. These skills enable them to articulate their vision and goals, build strong relationships with key stakeholders, and identify new opportunities for growth. By developing and leveraging these skills, entrepreneurs can increase the likelihood of success for their ventures.

TECHNIQUES FOR DEVELOPING INTERPERSONAL SKILLS

Developing strong interpersonal skills is a crucial aspect of success for entrepreneurs. Effective communication, relationship building, and networking are essential in building a business and reaching out to potential customers, clients, and partners. Here are some techniques that entrepreneurs can use to develop their interpersonal skills:

- **Active Listening:** Active listening is an essential skill that helps entrepreneurs better understand their customers, employees, and partners. It involves focusing on what the other person is saying, asking clarifying questions, and showing empathy. Active listening helps to build trust, improve communication, and enhance relationships.
- **Effective Storytelling:** Entrepreneurs must be able to tell their stories in a compelling and memorable way. Effective storytelling can be used to build a personal brand, connect with potential

customers, and secure investment. Using different storytelling techniques like using metaphors, anecdotes, and case studies to make their stories more engaging is essential.

- **Building a Personal Brand: A** strong personal brand can help entrepreneurs stand out from the crowd and build credibility with customers, investors, and partners. Building a personal brand involves developing a clear and consistent message that reflects the entrepreneur's values, vision, and strengths. Entrepreneurs can use social media, public speaking, and other forms of content marketing to build their personal brand.

- **Networking:** Networking is essential for entrepreneurs to build relationships and create new opportunities. Networking involves meeting new people, attending events, and engaging in online communities. Entrepreneurs can use networking to learn about industry trends, find new customers, and connect with potential investors and partners.

By developing these interpersonal skills, entrepreneurs can improve their communication, build stronger relationships, and create new opportunities for their business. It is essential for entrepreneurs to continuously work on developing their interpersonal skills to succeed in today's business environment.

ENTREPRENEURS WHO UTILIZED INTERPERSONAL SKILLS TO BUILD SUCCESSFUL BUSINESSES

There are many entrepreneurs who have utilized their interpersonal skills to build successful businesses.

Here are just a few examples:

- **Janice Bryant Howroyd**, founder of ActOne Group, a global staffing and consulting firm, built her business on strong relationships with clients and employees. She is known for her focus on personal connections and her ability to build trust and loyalty with both clients and employees.
- **Melissa Butler**, founder of The Lip Bar, a vegan and cruelty-free cosmetics company, built her business by telling her personal story and connecting with her customers on a personal level. She also utilizes social media to connect with her customers and build a community around her brand.
- **Jewel Burks Solomon**, founder of Partpic, a technology company that uses computer vision to simplify the process of finding industrial parts, built her business through networking and relationship-building. She connected with investors and other entrepreneurs through events and conferences, and utilized mentorship to help grow her business.

In each of these examples, the entrepreneurs utilized interpersonal skills such as networking, relationship-building, and effective communication to establish and grow successful businesses. By connecting with others and earning trust and loyalty, they were able to grow their customer base, attract investors, and build strong teams. These skills are essential for any entrepreneur looking to build a successful business, regardless of their background or industry.

Social Capital

Social capital refers to the set of relationships and connections individuals have with other people in their social networks, including family members, friends, colleagues, business associates, and other contacts. In the context of entrepreneurship, social capital plays an important role in helping entrepreneurs access what they need to start and grow their businesses.

Entrepreneurs with strong social capital can tap into their networks to obtain critical resources like financing, advice, expertise, and support that may be difficult to access through other means. For example, they may be able to secure investment capital from family members or close associates who are willing to take a chance on their business idea. They may also be able to obtain valuable advice and mentorship from individuals with relevant expertise or connect with potential customers and partners through their social networks.

Social capital can also provide important emotional support and encouragement for entrepreneurs. Building a business can be a challenging and isolating experience and having a supportive network of friends and associates who understand how to best support the entrepreneur can be invaluable in helping entrepreneurs navigate the ups and downs of the journey.

Building and leveraging social capital requires effective relationship-building skills, a willingness to invest time and energy in building and maintaining relationships, and a commitment to helping others in your network as well as seeking help for yourself.

THE ROLE OF NETWORKS, RELATIONSHIPS, AND RESOURCES IN CREATING AND SEIZING OPPORTUNITIES AS IT RELATES TO ENTREPRENEURSHIP

One of the key benefits of social capital is the access to information and resources. Entrepreneurs who have strong social networks are often better positioned to learn about new opportunities, industry trends, and potential customers. In addition, social capital can help entrepreneurs to build credibility and establish trust, which can be crucial in establishing partnerships and securing new business.

Another important aspect of social capital is the ability to build strong relationships with others. This can include partnerships with other businesses, collaborations with industry experts, and relationships with customers and clients. These relationships can be critical in establishing a strong reputation and building a loyal customer base. By leveraging their social networks, entrepreneurs can also gain access to new markets and expand their reach.

In addition to the benefits of social networks and relationships, social capital can also help entrepreneurs to build a strong reputation. By being seen as a valuable member of the community, entrepreneurs can establish themselves as experts in their field and gain the trust and respect of others. This can be especially important in industries where reputation and credibility are highly valued.

Overall, social capital plays a critical role in creating and seizing opportunities in entrepreneurship. By building strong networks, relationships, and resources, entrepreneurs can gain access to valuable information, resources, and opportunities that might not otherwise be available. Through these relationships, they can establish a strong reputation, build a loyal customer base, and expand their reach.

TYPES OF SOCIAL CAPITAL

Social capital refers to the resources that an individual can access through their network of social relationships. There are three types of social capital: structural, relational, and cognitive.

Structural social capital refers to the nature and number of connections that an individual has within their network. This includes the number of people in the network, the frequency and intensity of interactions, and the diversity of connections. Having a diverse network with strong ties to a variety of individuals and organizations can be a valuable source of information and resources.

Relational social capital refers to the strength and quality of the connections within an individual's network. Strong relationships are built on trust, reciprocity, and a sense of mutual respect. Entrepreneurs with strong relational social capital can rely on their network for support, advice, and access to resources.

Cognitive social capital refers to the knowledge and skills that an individual can access through their network. This includes expertise, information, and learning opportunities. Entrepreneurs with strong cognitive social capital can tap into the knowledge and experience of their network to improve their own skills and knowledge.

Each type of social capital is important for entrepreneurs because they each provide access to different resources and opportunities. Structural social capital can provide access to diverse resources and information, while relational social capital provides support and access to resources through strong relationships. Cognitive social capital provides access to knowledge and expertise.

TECHNIQUES FOR BUILDING SOCIAL CAPITAL

Building social capital is critical for entrepreneurs to succeed. Social capital refers to the value that can be derived from social networks and relationships, including access to resources and information. Here are four techniques that can help entrepreneurs build social capital:

- **Attending industry events**: Attending industry events such as conferences, workshops, and trade shows can help entrepreneurs meet other people in their field and build relationships with potential customers, partners, and investors. By being present and engaging with others, entrepreneurs can learn about new trends, challenges, and opportunities in their industry and get insights on how to improve their business.

- **Joining professional organizations**: Joining a professional organization can provide entrepreneurs with a network of like-minded individuals who can provide support, advice, and potential business opportunities. Professional organizations often host events, provide training and resources, and offer opportunities for entrepreneurs to get involved in advocacy efforts that can benefit their business and their industry.

- **Building a personal advisory board**: Building a personal advisory board of trusted advisors and mentors can provide entrepreneurs with valuable insights and perspectives on their business. Advisors can offer guidance on specific aspects of the business, provide feedback on new ideas, and offer referrals to other contacts in their network. Advisory boards can be made up of people from different backgrounds, industries, and experiences to provide diverse and well-rounded perspectives.

- **Creating strategic partnerships**: Forming partnerships with other businesses, organizations, and individuals can provide entrepreneurs with access to new resources, customers, and markets. By collaborating with others, entrepreneurs can share expertise, resources, and knowledge to create innovative solutions and achieve mutually beneficial goals. Strategic partnerships can also help entrepreneurs expand their network and build their reputation in their industry.

Building social capital requires entrepreneurs to be proactive and intentional about developing relationships and engaging with their industry and community. By investing in social capital, entrepreneurs can gain access to valuable resources and opportunities that can help them achieve their goals and grow their business.

Entrepreneurs Who Leveraged Social Capital to Advance Their Startup Companies

There are many examples of entrepreneurs who have successfully leveraged social capital to advance their startup companies.

One such example is **Erica Duignan Minnihan**, founder of 1000 Angels, a venture investment platform. Erica leveraged her social capital from her previous roles as a managing director at DreamIt Ventures and as a partner at the venture capital firm, New York Seed. She utilized her network of connections to secure investments and connect entrepreneurs with angel investors.

Another example is **Kathryn Finney**, founder of digitalundivided, an organization that supports Black and Latinx women entrepreneurs in the tech industry. Kathryn leveraged her social capital as a respected thought leader and advocate for underrepresented founders to build a community of entrepreneurs, investors, and corporate partners. This enabled her to secure funding and partnerships to support her mission.

A third example is **Stacy Brown-Philpot**, former CEO of TaskRabbit, an online and mobile marketplace that connects users with local freelancers. Stacy leveraged her social capital from her previous role as an executive at Google to secure investment funding and partnerships with companies such as IKEA.

These examples demonstrate how entrepreneurs have leveraged social capital to build their businesses. By building strong relationships and networks, these entrepreneurs were able to access resources, secure funding, and build strategic partnerships, all of which were critical to the success of their ventures.

Summary

Confidence, risk-taking, interpersonal skills, and social capital are crucial components of entrepreneurial success.

Confidence is important for entrepreneurs because it provides the foundation for taking risks and pursuing opportunities. A confident entrepreneur is more likely to take risks and is better equipped to handle setbacks and failures. Techniques for building confidence include positive self-talk, visualization, seeking feedback, and taking action.

Risk-taking is an essential part of entrepreneurship because it creates opportunities for innovation and growth. The types of risks that entrepreneurs face include financial, reputational, strategic, and psychological. Techniques for managing risk include conducting market research, diversifying, developing contingency plans, and seeking advice from experts.

Interpersonal skills are crucial for entrepreneurs because they facilitate effective communication, networking, and relationship-building. Techniques for developing interpersonal skills include active listening, effective storytelling, building a personal brand, and networking.

Social capital, which encompasses networks, relationships, and resources, is also critical for entrepreneurial success. Types of social capital include structural, relational, and cognitive. Techniques for building social capital include attending industry events, joining professional organizations, building a personal advisory board, and creating strategic partnerships.

Overall, these four components of entrepreneurial success are interrelated and build upon one another. A confident entrepreneur is more likely to take risks, and strong interpersonal skills and social capital can provide the support and resources necessary to help an entrepreneur navigate and manage those risks. Successful entrepreneurs must balance these four components and be able to leverage them effectively to seize opportunities and create a thriving business.

9. Seeing Entrepreneurially

An entrepreneur is someone who can see the opportunity in every situation, even when it's disguised as a problem.

Reid Hoffman
Co-founder of LinkedIn

Successful entrepreneurs introduce a product or service that satisfies customer needs in a better way than competitors at a price that is greater than the cost of creating and delivering that product or service.

To understand how to fulfill customer needs at an attractive price, four areas are critical to assess: *industry condition, industry status, macroeconomic change,* and *competition.*

The Opportunity Analysis Canvas

Emphasis on "Part II – Seeing Entrepreneurially"

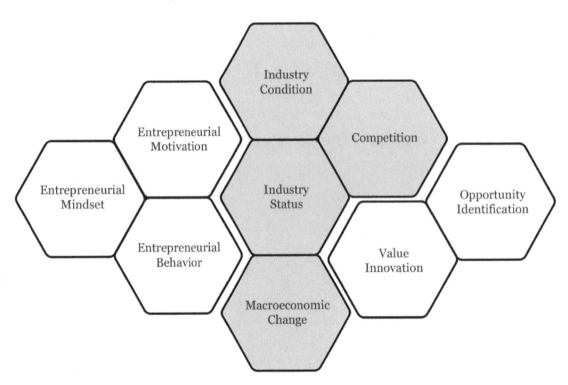

INDUSTRY CONDITION

Assessing the condition of an industry is crucial in identifying opportunities for entrepreneurs. Industry conditions can present opportunities for new entrants to create disruptive innovations or to address unmet needs in the market. A key aspect of assessing industry conditions is identifying factors such as the life cycle of the industry, market saturation, and regulatory environment. Life cycle analysis can reveal stages of industry development where there is a need for innovation or new product or service offerings. Market saturation analysis can identify areas where new entrants can disrupt the market by offering a unique value proposition. Assessing regulatory environments can reveal areas of opportunity where regulations can be leveraged to create a competitive advantage.

INDUSTRY STATUS

Understanding the status of an industry can help entrepreneurs identify areas of unmet needs and areas where there may be potential for growth. Industry status analysis includes examining factors such as market size, growth rate, and consumer preferences. A key aspect of industry status analysis is identifying areas where there is a gap in the market or an unmet need that can be addressed through innovation or new product or service offerings. Entrepreneurs must also keep a watchful eye on industry trends and changes in consumer preferences to ensure that they remain competitive.

MACROECONOMIC CHANGE

Macro-economic change is another critical area to assess when identifying opportunities for entrepreneurs. Macroeconomic change can present opportunities for new product or service offerings or new market entrants. Macro-economic changes may include changes in interest rates, inflation, foreign exchange rates, and shifts in global trade patterns. Entrepreneurs must keep a watchful eye on these macroeconomic changes as they can have a significant impact on the viability of new businesses.

COMPETITION

Assessing the competition is a critical aspect of identifying opportunities for entrepreneurs. Understanding the competition can reveal areas of unmet needs or areas where competitors have a weak value proposition. Key aspects of assessing competition include identifying strengths and weaknesses of competitors, evaluating their pricing strategies and distribution channels, and analyzing their marketing and advertising campaigns. Entrepreneurs must identify their unique value proposition and how it can be leveraged to create a competitive advantage.

SUMMARY

Seeing entrepreneurially is crucial for identifying opportunities for new product or service offerings, new market entrants, and disruptive innovations. Assessing industry conditions, industry status, macroeconomic change, and competition can provide valuable insights for entrepreneurs to identify areas of unmet needs, market gaps, and opportunities for growth. Successful entrepreneurs must see opportunities where others see only obstacles or limitations. By leveraging the insights gained from the assessment of the four areas outlined in this chapter, entrepreneurs can develop unique value propositions, disruptive innovations, and competitive advantages that will set them apart from their competitors.

10. Industry Condition

Our idea is to serve everybody, including people with little money.

Ingvar Kamprad

Founder of IKEA

After examining entrepreneurial mindset, motivation, and behavior, the next step in exploring entrepreneurial opportunities is evaluating *industry condition*. We can examine the rules of competition within an industry. This helps entrepreneurs to decide what industries they may want to enter and which ones they may want to avoid. For those industries they do choose to enter, entrepreneurs can better anticipate the opportunities and challenges therein.

Understanding the *knowledge conditions* and *demand conditions*, the two core segments of industry condition, provides insights into the attractiveness of an industry for new entrants. With this understanding, aspiring entrepreneurs can determine if, and how, to compete effectively within their chosen industry.

The Opportunity Analysis Canvas

Emphasis on "Industry Condition"

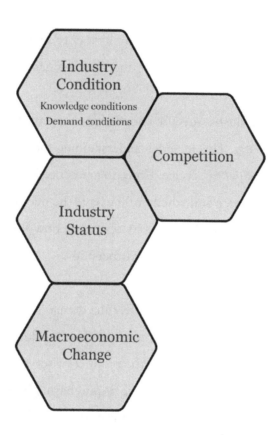

Two Core Segments of Industry Condition

Industry condition is an important aspect of evaluating entrepreneurial opportunities. It involves analyzing the rules of competition within an industry and the market environment where a product or service will be offered. Knowledge conditions and demand conditions are two core segments of industry condition that are essential for entrepreneurs to consider when evaluating the attractiveness of an industry for new entrants.

Knowledge conditions refer to the industry-specific knowledge necessary for entrepreneurs to operate effectively within their chosen industry. This includes understanding the technologies, techniques, and processes required to produce a product or service. Entrepreneurs need to assess the level of knowledge required to create their product or service and whether they have the necessary expertise to be successful. If entrepreneurs lack the required knowledge, they need to determine how they will acquire it, such as through training, hiring experienced staff, or forming strategic partnerships.

Demand conditions refer to the external factors that affect the demand for a product or service in the market. Entrepreneurs need to assess the current demand for their product or service, whether there is potential for growth, and whether they can provide their product or service at a competitive price. Entrepreneurs need to research their target customers, their purchasing habits, and their preferences to determine if there is sufficient demand to support their business.

In evaluating both knowledge conditions and demand conditions, entrepreneurs can determine the level of competition within their chosen industry. They can assess whether there are many existing players, whether they are well-established, and if they have a strong market position. This information can help entrepreneurs decide if they can compete effectively within the industry, and if there are opportunities for profitability.

In summary, evaluating knowledge conditions and demand conditions is crucial for entrepreneurs to determine the attractiveness of an industry for new entrants. Entrepreneurs need to analyze the level of knowledge required to operate effectively within their chosen industry, and whether there is a market need for their product or service. They also need to consider the level of competition within the industry and the opportunities for growth and profitability. By assessing these two core segments of industry condition, entrepreneurs can make informed decisions about entering a new industry and competing effectively within it.

Knowledge Conditions

Knowledge conditions refer to the degree of understanding, research, and development of knowledge in a particular industry or field. It is crucial for entrepreneurs to understand the knowledge conditions of their chosen industry, as this information can determine the feasibility of their business idea, and the extent to which it can be developed into a successful enterprise.

A thorough understanding of the knowledge conditions within an industry can help entrepreneurs identify new trends and potential areas for innovation, enabling them to create products or services that are unique and better than existing options. Knowledge conditions can include factors such as the level of research and development, the number of patents filed, the expertise of employees, and the availability of resources for knowledge acquisition.

For example, in the technology industry, the knowledge conditions are constantly evolving, with new advancements and innovations happening at a rapid pace. This makes it imperative for entrepreneurs in this field to stay informed of new developments and adapt their business strategies accordingly.

In contrast, industries with less dynamic knowledge conditions, such as the real estate industry, may offer fewer opportunities for innovation and require a more conservative approach to entrepreneurship.

In summary, knowledge conditions are important for entrepreneurs to consider when evaluating industry condition because they help to identify the degree to which an industry is suited to the entrepreneur's expertise, and the level of innovation and potential for growth that can be achieved in the chosen industry. Entrepreneurs need to be aware of the knowledge conditions of their chosen industry to identify new areas of opportunity and stay up to date with the latest trends and advancements, enabling them to create products or services that are more effective, efficient, and better than existing options.

FACTORS THAT CONTRIBUTE TO KNOWLEDGE CONDITIONS

Knowledge conditions are a crucial aspect to consider when evaluating the feasibility of starting a business in a particular industry. The factors that contribute to the knowledge conditions can vary depending on the specific industry.

One important factor is proprietary knowledge, which refers to knowledge that is owned and protected by a company. This may include patents, trade secrets, copyrights, or trademarks, and it gives the company a competitive advantage over firms that do not have access to this knowledge. For example, a software company that has developed a unique algorithm to perform a certain function may have proprietary knowledge that is valuable to customers, making it difficult for competitors to replicate their product.

Another factor that contributes to knowledge conditions is specialized skills. Some industries require specialized skills and expertise to be successful. For example, a company in the healthcare industry may require specialized medical knowledge and training to develop and market their products. This can be a barrier to entry for new businesses, as they may not have access to the specialized skills required to be competitive in the industry.

Research and development is also a key factor in creating knowledge conditions. Industries that require high levels of research and development, such as the technology industry, demand a significant investment in knowledge acquisition to be successful. This includes not only developing new products, but also improving existing ones, staying up to date with industry trends and developments, and investing in new technologies.

Overall, knowledge conditions are an important factor for entrepreneurs to consider when evaluating the feasibility of starting a business in a particular industry. Companies that have access to proprietary knowledge, specialized skills, and research and development capabilities are likely to have a competitive advantage over those that do not. By understanding the knowledge conditions within an industry, entrepreneurs can better assess the opportunities and challenges they may face and make informed decisions about whether or not to enter the market.

HOW KNOWLEDGE CONDITIONS AFFECT MARKET COMPETITION AND PROFITABILITY

Knowledge conditions can significantly impact market competition and profitability in entrepreneurship. When an industry has high-knowledge conditions, there are typically a limited number of firms with proprietary knowledge, specialized skills, and research and development capabilities. These firms have an advantage over competitors because they are better equipped to develop and deliver products or services that meet the needs of the market. As a result, they are likely to have higher profits and a stronger competitive position.

However, high-knowledge conditions can also create barriers to entry for new firms. Aspiring entrepreneurs may struggle to enter the market because they lack the specialized knowledge or resources to compete with established firms. This can lead to a less competitive market, which may result in higher prices for consumers and decreased innovation.

On the other hand, low-knowledge conditions can create opportunities for new entrants to enter the market. When there are few proprietary knowledge, specialized skills, or research and development capabilities, there is less of a competitive advantage for established firms. This may lead to a more open and competitive market, which can benefit consumers with increased innovation and lower prices.

It is also worth noting that knowledge conditions can change over time. For example, a firm that has proprietary knowledge or specialized skills may lose its competitive advantage if its knowledge becomes more widely available or if other firms develop similar capabilities. As such, entrepreneurs need to continuously monitor and adapt to changes in knowledge conditions in their industry to remain competitive and profitable.

Remember, knowledge conditions play a critical role in market competition and profitability in entrepreneurship. Entrepreneurs need to understand the knowledge conditions of their industry to identify opportunities and challenges, determine the feasibility of entering the market, and develop effective strategies for competing and thriving in their industry.

INDUSTRIES WITH STRONG KNOWLEDGE CONDITIONS

There are several industries with strong knowledge conditions that require specialized skills, extensive research, and a deep understanding of the market to succeed. Here are some examples:

- **Aerospace:** The aerospace industry is a high-tech industry that requires a lot of specialized knowledge and expertise. Companies in this industry need to have strong research and development capabilities to innovate and stay ahead of competitors. The industry is highly competitive, with many large players vying for market share.

- **Biotechnology:** The biotechnology industry involves the use of living organisms and biological processes to develop new products, such as drugs and medical devices. The industry is highly regulated and requires significant investment in research and development to bring a product to market. Companies in this industry need to have specialized knowledge and expertise to compete effectively.

- **Financial Services:** The financial services industry is heavily regulated and requires specialized knowledge and expertise to navigate the complex regulatory environment. Companies in this industry need to have strong research capabilities and be able to anticipate changes in the market to stay ahead of the competition.

- **Pharmaceuticals:** The pharmaceutical industry is highly regulated and requires significant investment in research and development to bring a new drug to market. Companies in this industry need to have specialized knowledge and expertise to compete effectively and remain competitive.

- **Software:** The software industry is highly competitive and requires specialized skills to develop new products and stay ahead of the curve. Companies in this industry need to have a deep understanding of their customers' needs and be able to anticipate market trends to stay ahead of the competition.

These industries require companies to have a strong understanding of the market, a deep knowledge of their customers' needs, and the ability to innovate and stay ahead of the curve. Success in these industries requires a strong focus on research and development, specialized skills, and a willingness to invest in new technologies and processes to rise above their competitors.

Demand Conditions

Demand conditions refer to the economic factors that determine the overall demand for a product or service in a particular industry. These conditions influence the number of buyers, the extent to which buyers are willing to pay for a product, and the frequency with which they buy it. In essence, demand conditions provide entrepreneurs with insights into the potential of a market and can determine how successful they are in creating and delivering products and services to customers.

Demand conditions are influenced by a wide variety of factors. One of the most important is the size and growth rate of the market, which helps entrepreneurs determine the overall demand for a product or service. For example, a growing market with a large customer base is typically more attractive to entrepreneurs than a stagnant or declining market with fewer potential customers.

Other important factors that contribute to demand conditions include the level of competition within an industry, the price customers are willing to pay for a product or service, and the extent to which customers are loyal to particular brands or products. In addition, economic conditions, such as the availability of disposable income and the overall economic health of a particular region or country, can significantly impact demand conditions and affect the overall success of an entrepreneurial venture.

Entrepreneurs who can identify and respond to changing demand conditions are often more successful than those who do not. For example, an entrepreneur who can identify a new trend in consumer demands, such as an increased interest in healthy eating or sustainable products, may be able to create a successful new product or service that meets these needs. Similarly, an entrepreneur who can identify and respond to changes in economic conditions, such as a recession or economic boom, may be able to adjust their pricing, marketing, or other strategies in order to maintain profitability.

In essence, demand conditions are a critical factor in the success of any entrepreneurial venture. Entrepreneurs who are able to effectively identify and respond to changing demand conditions are more likely to create successful products and services, build strong customer relationships, and achieve long-term profitability.

FACTORS THAT CONTRIBUTE TO DEMAND CONDITIONS

Demand conditions are an important aspect of industry condition that entrepreneurs must consider when evaluating opportunities. Demand conditions are the set of factors that influence the demand for a product or service within an industry. These factors include customer preferences, demographics, economic trends, and other market forces that can affect the sales of a product or service.

One of the most important factors in demand conditions is customer preferences. Entrepreneurs need to understand the needs and wants of their potential customers and how their product or service can meet those needs in a unique and valuable way. For example, if a new restaurant is opening in a specific area, entrepreneurs need to determine the type of cuisine that would be popular in that area and create a menu that offers that cuisine to attract local customers.

Demographics is another important factor that entrepreneurs need to consider. For example, the age, income, and cultural background of a target market can have a significant impact on the demand for a particular product or service. Entrepreneurs need to analyze these factors and tailor their offerings to the specific needs of their target customers.

Economic trends is another important factor that entrepreneurs need to consider. For example, changes in the overall economy, such as a recession or an economic boom, can affect the demand for a particular product or service. Entrepreneurs need to monitor economic trends and adjust their offerings accordingly. They may also need to adjust pricing, marketing strategies, and other aspects of their business to remain competitive in changing economic conditions.

Other market forces such as changes in technology, industry trends, and consumer behavior can also affect demand conditions. Entrepreneurs need to stay up to date on these changes and adapt their offerings to stay competitive.

In summary, demand conditions are the set of factors that determine the demand for a product or service in a specific industry. Entrepreneurs must consider customer preferences, demographics, economic trends, and other market forces when evaluating the demand conditions of a potential opportunity. By understanding these factors and adapting their offerings accordingly, entrepreneurs can create products and services that meet the needs of their target customers and achieve success in their industry.

HOW DEMAND CONDITIONS AFFECT MARKET COMPETITION AND PROFITABILITY

Demand conditions play a crucial role in the success of a business. The strength of customer demand and the overall market demand for a product or service can greatly impact competition and profitability in an industry. When demand is high, businesses can charge higher prices and increase their profit margins. Conversely, when demand is low, businesses may need to lower prices to stay competitive or even exit the market altogether.

High-demand conditions can also lead to increased competition as more businesses enter the market to take advantage of the opportunity. This can result in a more crowded market and price wars among competitors, leading to decreased profitability for all businesses involved. However, high demand can also spur innovation and differentiation as businesses try to stand out in a crowded market and attract more customers.

On the other hand, low-demand conditions can lead to a reduction in competition as businesses exit the market, leaving more opportunities for those that remain. However, low demand can also lead to decreased innovation and fewer new entrants, as businesses may not see it as a viable market opportunity.

Another factor that affects demand conditions is the overall state of the economy. In a strong economy, consumers tend to have more disposable income, which can lead to increased demand for certain products and services. However, in a weak economy, consumers may be more price-sensitive and less willing to spend money on non-essential items.

Understanding demand conditions is crucial for entrepreneurs looking to enter or compete in a particular market. By analyzing customer preferences, demographics, economic trends, and other factors that impact demand, entrepreneurs can make informed decisions about pricing, product development, and marketing strategies. By doing so, they can increase their chances of success and profitability in their chosen industry.

EXAMPLES OF DEMAND CONDITIONS

Demand conditions play a significant role in shaping the competitiveness and profitability of industries. Here are some examples of industries with strong demand conditions:

- **Energy:** The demand for energy is influenced by economic and environmental factors, as well as changing consumer preferences. The energy industry is highly regulated, with significant barriers to entry for new players. As a result, established companies often dominate the market.

- **Fashion:** The fashion industry is highly influenced by trends, consumer preferences, and economic factors. The success of fashion brands often depends on their ability to anticipate and adapt to these factors while differentiating themselves from competitors.

- **Food and Beverage:** The food and beverage industry is highly dependent on consumer preferences, which are often driven by factors such as taste, health, and convenience. There is a constant need for innovation in this industry, as consumers are always looking for new and exciting products.

- **Health care:** The demand for health care products and services is driven by demographic factors, such as an aging population and the increasing prevalence of chronic diseases. As a result, the health care industry is highly competitive, with large, established players dominating the market.

- **Technology:** The tech industry has a high demand for innovative products and services due to the constant need for better, faster, and more efficient technologies. This creates an environment of fierce competition and high barriers to entry for new startups.

In all these industries, entrepreneurs must carefully evaluate the demand conditions and identify areas where they can offer a unique value proposition to customers. This may involve developing innovative products, identifying new market niches, or differentiating themselves from established competitors. By understanding the demand conditions within an industry, entrepreneurs can position themselves to succeed and create long-term value for their customers and stakeholders.

EVALUATING INDUSTRY ATTRACTIVENESS BEFORE ENTERING A MARKET

Before entering a market, it is essential for entrepreneurs to evaluate the attractiveness of the industry to ensure a greater likelihood of success. This evaluation requires careful consideration of the industry's knowledge and demand conditions, as well as other factors such as macroeconomic changes, competition, and market dynamics.

Evaluating industry attractiveness helps entrepreneurs identify opportunities that offer a competitive advantage and avoid markets that may be too crowded or not profitable. This analysis enables entrepreneurs to understand the industry's potential for growth, identify potential threats and risks, and assess the market's overall potential. By assessing industry attractiveness, entrepreneurs can make informed decisions about their business strategies and investments, reducing the likelihood of making costly mistakes.

Moreover, evaluating industry attractiveness helps entrepreneurs understand their target customers, identify their needs and preferences, and develop products and services that meet those needs. By focusing on markets with strong demand conditions, entrepreneurs can better anticipate their customers' requirements and deliver more innovative and valuable products or services that satisfy their expectations. They can also gain a competitive edge by offering unique and specialized products or services that address a specific customer niche.

Furthermore, assessing industry attractiveness also helps entrepreneurs to determine the level of competition in the market. By evaluating the level of competition, entrepreneurs can identify their competitors' strengths and weaknesses and devise effective strategies for gaining a competitive advantage.

156

This analysis can also help entrepreneurs anticipate future competition and take steps to counter their actions proactively.

Finally, evaluating industry attractiveness helps entrepreneurs identify potential risks and challenges associated with the market. These include economic, social, regulatory, or technological factors that could affect the business's long-term viability. By identifying these risks, entrepreneurs can develop contingency plans and take necessary precautions to protect their businesses against potential threats.

In summary, evaluating industry attractiveness is crucial for entrepreneurs who want to enter a new market successfully. By understanding the industry's knowledge and demand conditions, assessing competition levels, and identifying potential risks and opportunities, entrepreneurs can make informed decisions about their business strategies, investments, and operations. This analysis provides entrepreneurs with a solid foundation for developing innovative and valuable products or services that meet customer needs and outcompete their rivals.

HOW KNOWLEDGE CONDITIONS AND DEMAND CONDITIONS HELP DETERMINE INDUSTRY ATTRACTIVENESS

Entrepreneurs face a significant risk when entering a new industry, which highlights the need to understand industry conditions. Industry attractiveness can be evaluated by analyzing knowledge conditions and demand conditions. By examining these two factors, entrepreneurs can determine if an industry is suitable for their business and if they can compete effectively within it.

Evaluating industry attractiveness before entering a market is essential to reduce the risk of failure. Entrepreneurs need to conduct thorough research to understand industry conditions and assess their ability to compete effectively within an industry. Knowledge and demand conditions provide entrepreneurs with valuable insights into industry attractiveness, helping them determine if they can meet the requirements for success in the industry. By evaluating these two core segments, entrepreneurs can determine the potential for profitability and decide whether to enter the industry or not. Overall, entrepreneurs who can evaluate industry attractiveness effectively have a greater chance of success.

How Select Tools are Valuable for Evaluating Industry Attractiveness

Tools such as Porter's Five Forces and SWOT analysis can be valuable for evaluating industry attractiveness, as they provide a systematic framework for analyzing an industry's competitive environment and identifying key opportunities and threats.

Porter's Five Forces is a framework that evaluates an industry's competitive forces to determine its attractiveness. The five forces include the threat of new entrants, the bargaining power of buyers, the bargaining power of suppliers, the threat of substitutes, and the intensity of competitive rivalry. By evaluating these forces, entrepreneurs can determine the potential profitability of the industry and identify the key factors that will determine their success.

SWOT analysis, on the other hand, is a tool used to identify an organization's strengths, weaknesses, opportunities, and threats. By analyzing these four factors, entrepreneurs can identify their competitive advantages, potential weaknesses, key opportunities, and major threats to their success. This information can then be used to develop a strategic plan for entering the market and competing effectively.

When evaluating industry attractiveness using Porter's Five Forces and SWOT analysis, entrepreneurs should consider a range of factors, such as market size, growth rate, profitability, competitive dynamics, customer needs, and technological trends. They should also consider factors such as regulatory environment, cultural norms, and social trends that may impact their ability to succeed in the market.

For example, a startup looking to enter the online retail market could use Porter's Five Forces to evaluate the industry's competitive environment. They could assess the threat of new entrants by looking at the barriers to entry in the market, such as economies of scale and network effects. They could also evaluate the bargaining power of buyers and suppliers, as well as the threat of substitutes, to understand the market's profitability potential. Using SWOT analysis, the startup could identify their competitive advantages, such as their unique product offerings or superior customer service, as well as potential weaknesses, such as a lack of brand recognition or limited financial resources. This information could be used to develop a strategic plan for entering the market and competing effectively.

In summary, tools such as Porter's Five Forces and SWOT analysis can provide valuable insights into industry attractiveness and help entrepreneurs identify key opportunities and threats in the market. By carefully evaluating these factors, entrepreneurs can develop a strong understanding of the industry and develop effective strategies for success.

How FiscalNote Used Knowledge Conditions and Demand Conditions in Their Success

FiscalNote is a Washington, D.C.-based technology company that provides businesses and organizations with real-time legislative and regulatory data. The company was founded in 2013 by Tim Hwang, Gerald Yao, and Jonathan Chen, all of whom were frustrated with the lack of transparency and access to government data. They saw an opportunity to use technology to provide businesses and organizations with the information they needed to stay up to date on legislative and regulatory developments.

FiscalNote has leveraged knowledge conditions to provide value to its customers. The company has developed proprietary algorithms that collect and analyze data from a variety of sources, including federal and state legislative websites, regulatory agencies, news outlets, and social media. FiscalNote's algorithms can detect and interpret complex patterns within the data, allowing the company to provide its customers with real-time information about legislative and regulatory developments that affect the business.

FiscalNote has also focused on demand conditions to grow its customer base and achieve success. The company has identified that businesses and organizations need access to real-time legislative and regulatory data to make informed decisions. The demand for such data has grown in recent years due to increased government regulation and the need for businesses to stay informed about changes that could impact their operations.

To meet this demand, FiscalNote has developed a suite of products that provides businesses and organizations access to the legislative and regulatory data they need. These products include FiscalNote State, FiscalNote Federal, and FiscalNote Advocacy, which provide businesses and organizations with access to real-time data, analytics, and insights about legislative and regulatory developments at the state and federal levels.

Moreover, FiscalNote has expanded its market reach by acquiring other companies with complementary products and expertise, such as data visualization and artificial intelligence. In 2019, FiscalNote acquired AI and data visualization company, AIQ, for an undisclosed sum. FiscalNote also acquired a legislative and regulatory data provider, CQ Roll Call, in 2018 for $180 million.

With proprietary technology, knowledge conditions, and an understanding of demand conditions, FiscalNote has been able to successfully grow its customer base and expand its market reach. The company has received several rounds of funding, including a $180 million funding round in 2018 led by the Japanese telecommunications company SoftBank.

FiscalNote's success has shown that entrepreneurs who understand knowledge and demand conditions and can develop innovative solutions to meet the needs of their customers can achieve significant growth and success.

Summary

In conclusion, understanding industry conditions is crucial for entrepreneurial success. Two core segments of industry conditions, knowledge conditions and demand conditions, can help entrepreneurs assess the attractiveness of an industry for new entrants. Knowledge conditions refer to the presence and availability of proprietary knowledge, specialized skills, and research and development. Demand conditions refer to customer preferences, demographics, and economic trends.

Knowledge conditions and demand conditions are both critical factors in determining the attractiveness of an industry. They can affect market competition and profitability, as they influence the ease of entry, level of competition, and potential for growth. Knowledge conditions can be a barrier to entry, limiting the number of players in the market, whereas demand conditions may indicate an untapped market opportunity.

To summarize, before entering a market, entrepreneurs must evaluate industry attractiveness by analyzing knowledge conditions and demand conditions. Tools such as Porter's Five Forces and SWOT analysis can help entrepreneurs identify market trends, understand competition, and assess their strengths and weaknesses.

Entrepreneurial success is not only about having a great idea or being passionate about a product or service. Entrepreneurs need to evaluate industry conditions to determine if there is a gap in the market that can be filled. Knowledge conditions and demand conditions are critical factors that need to be considered when assessing the attractiveness of an industry. By evaluating industry conditions, entrepreneurs can make informed decisions on whether to enter a market, how to compete effectively, and how to maximize profitability.

11. Industry Status

If General Motors had kept up with technology like the computer industry has,

we would all be driving $25 cars that got 1,000 miles per gallon.

Bill Gates

Co-founder of Microsoft

With industry conditions addressing the knowledge and demand factors, it's important to understand *industry lifecycle* and *industry structure* as the key components of *industry status*. By studying industry status, aspiring entrepreneurs can assess an industry's timeliness for new entrepreneurial entrants.

We'll discuss how industries evolve and what happens as new competitors emerge. I'll also help you recognize the timelines and windows of opportunity that are going to maximize your success within an industry.

The Opportunity Analysis Canvas

Emphasis on "Industry Status"

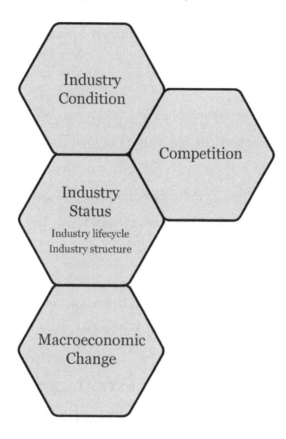

Industry status refers to the current state of a specific industry in terms of its lifecycle and structure. The industry lifecycle model is a framework that describes the various stages of an industry, from its inception to its eventual decline. Industry structure, on the other hand, refers to the competitive environment within an industry, including the number and size of competitors, the nature of the products or services being offered, and the degree of market concentration.

167

As an aspiring entrepreneur, understanding the industry status of the market you are interested in is important to identify the potential opportunities and threats. Industry status can provide a critical foundation for strategic planning and decision-making. By examining the stage of the industry lifecycle and the competitive structure, an entrepreneur can better evaluate the potential risks and rewards of entering that market.

For example, if an industry is in the early stages of its lifecycle, it may offer attractive opportunities for innovative and disruptive products or services. Similarly, if an industry has a fragmented competitive structure, with many small players, it may present a chance for new entrants to gain market share and become significant players. Conversely, if an industry is in the later stages of its lifecycle, or if there is a high degree of market concentration among a few dominant players, it may be challenging for a new entrant to compete effectively.

Understanding the industry status helps entrepreneurs in better assessing the feasibility of their business ideas, designing strategies for entering the market, and competing effectively to create value for customers.

THE IMPORTANCE OF UNDERSTANDING INDUSTRY LIFECYCLE AND INDUSTRY STRUCTURE AS THEY RELATE TO ENTREPRENEURSHIP

Understanding industry lifecycle and industry structure is crucial for entrepreneurs who want to identify opportunities and anticipate changes within an industry. Industry lifecycle refers to the stages that an industry goes through, which are the introduction phase, growth phase, maturity phase, and decline phase. Each stage presents unique opportunities and challenges for entrepreneurs.

As previously stated, industry structure refers to the number and size of companies in the industry, the extent of product differentiation, and the level of barriers to entry. Industry structure affects the intensity of competition in the industry, the level of innovation, and the overall profitability.

Understanding industry lifecycle and industry structure can help entrepreneurs make informed decisions about which industries to enter and how to compete effectively within them. For example, entrepreneurs may choose to enter an industry during its growth phase when there is high demand and significant opportunities for innovation. Alternatively, they may choose to enter a mature industry and differentiate their products or services to stand out from competitors. By understanding industry structure, entrepreneurs can also identify gaps in the market and areas where they can carve out a niche.

Moreover, entrepreneurs who anticipate changes in industry lifecycle and structure can position themselves for success. For example, if an industry is entering the decline phase, entrepreneurs may choose to pivot to a new industry with more growth potential. If an industry is becoming more consolidated, entrepreneurs may choose to merge with other companies or seek strategic partnerships to increase their bargaining power.

In conclusion, understanding industry lifecycle and structure is crucial for entrepreneurs who want to identify opportunities, anticipate changes, and compete effectively within their chosen industries. By evaluating industry status, entrepreneurs can make informed decisions about where to invest their resources and how to position themselves for long-term success.

THE STAGES OF THE INDUSTRY LIFECYCLE

The industry lifecycle is a model used to explain how industries evolve over time, and the stages that industries typically go through. Understanding the different stages of the industry lifecycle is critical to successful entrepreneurship, as it helps entrepreneurs identify windows of opportunity and determine the most appropriate strategies to succeed in a particular industry.

The four stages of industry lifecycle are:

1. **Introduction:** The introduction stage marks the launch of a new product or service to the market. Sales are low, and high uncertainty and risk define this stage. Entrepreneurs may need to invest in research and development and marketing to build brand awareness and demand. Typically, few firms operate in the industry, and the market is undefined. High investment and high risk are characteristic of this stage. The product is new, and consumers are not yet aware of it, so sales may be slow, and profits low. The duration of the introduction stage varies based on the product's complexity and market entry barriers. This stage presents an opportunity for entrepreneurs to offer new products or services that meet consumers' needs. The introduction stage is associated with intense competition, low barriers to entry, and considerable uncertainty.

2. **Growth:** During the growth stage, demand for a product or service increases rapidly, which leads to the emergence of competitors. Entrepreneurs who enter the market during this stage focus on building brand awareness, market share, and investing in research and development to enhance their product or service offerings. Growth during this stage may require raising capital to expand operations and satisfy growing demand. In the growth stage, companies build market share and the number of competitors increases. The focus is on product differentiation and customer retention,

170

resulting in high marketing and advertising expenses. This stage sees an accelerated increase in demand and a rise in sales and profits, shifting the focus to production and cost efficiency to keep up with demand. The growth stage can last from a few years to over a decade, depending on the market conditions.

During the growth stage, demand for products and services increases quickly, creating a favorable market for entrepreneurs. While competition is not as high as it is in the introduction stage, barriers to entry may be greater and established firms may have a significant advantage due to economies of scale and brand recognition. Entrepreneurs who enter the market during this stage must be prepared to scale their operations rapidly and effectively to keep up with demand. Access to significant financial resources is necessary, and the ability to recruit and retain skilled employees is critical. A successful entrepreneur in the growth stage will focus on developing innovative marketing strategies and building a loyal customer base while optimizing production and supply chain management to maintain profitability.

3. **Maturity:** In the maturity stage of the industry lifecycle, demand growth slows down and competition becomes even more intense. Entrepreneurs entering the market at this stage may focus on cutting costs, streamlining operations, and investing in new product offerings to continue to grow their revenue. Maturity is the third stage in the industry lifecycle, characterized by market saturation, cost reduction, and operational efficiency. Pricing pressures increase as profit margins decline. Product differentiation becomes increasingly difficult in this stage, and firms must focus on increasing operational efficiency to maintain market position. The maturity stage can last for several decades, during which the market stabilizes and growth rates slow. Intense competition characterizes the market, and product differentiation becomes critical to maintaining market share. Entrepreneurs

who enter the market at this stage must differentiate their offerings from established firms and focus on niche markets or innovative business models. The cost of entry may be lower than in earlier stages, but the potential for high returns may also be lower. Success in this stage depends on an entrepreneur's ability to manage costs and optimize operations. Entrepreneurs may also need to consider merging with or acquiring other companies to gain a competitive edge. In the maturity stage, market conditions can be challenging for new entrants, but opportunities may exist for those who can identify and capitalize on unmet needs or gaps in the market.

4. **Decline:** The decline stage is defined by a drop in demand and increased competition from substitute products or services. Entrepreneurs who enter the market at this point should concentrate on diversifying their offerings or discovering new markets. Some may not want to enter the market at all at this stage, and those already in it may consider exiting the sector entirely. This decline stage is the final stage of the industry lifecycle and is characterized by negative growth and businesses leaving the market. At this stage, market saturation is complete and demand for goods or services decreases. Companies must choose whether to reposition themselves or leave the industry. Weaker firms exit and the market share of stronger firms grows. Sales and profits decrease due to increased competition, market saturation, or changing consumer preferences. The decline stage can last until the product becomes obsolete or is replaced by a new technology or product.

In summary, the stage of an industry's lifecycle has important implications for entrepreneurship. Entrepreneurs must be prepared to invest heavily in the introduction stage, scale their operations quickly in the growth stage, differentiate their offerings in the maturity stage, and focus on cost-cutting and efficiency in the decline stage. By understanding the stage of the industry lifecycle and the implications for entrepreneurship, aspiring entrepreneurs can make informed decisions about the opportunities and challenges that lie ahead.

Industry Structure

Industry structure refers to the composition, organization, and characteristics of firms within a particular market or industry. The structure of an industry can significantly impact the behavior and performance of firms operating within it.

One important aspect of industry structure is the level of competition among firms. Highly competitive industries typically have many firms operating within them, all vying for market share and profit. In contrast, industries with low levels of competition may be dominated by a few large firms, leading to reduced competitive pressures and potential barriers to entry for new firms.

Another aspect of industry structure is the degree of product differentiation. In industries where products or services are highly differentiated, firms may be able to charge higher prices and may face reduced competition from substitute products or services. In contrast, in industries where products or services are more homogeneous, firms may be forced to compete more on price and may face increased competition from substitutes.

The degree of vertical integration is another important aspect of industry structure. Vertical integration refers to the degree to which firms control the entire supply chain, from raw materials to finished products. In some industries, firms may be highly vertically integrated, controlling all aspects of the production and distribution process. In contrast, other industries may be more fragmented, with many firms specializing in specific aspects of the supply chain.

The regulatory environment is another important factor in industry structure. Industries that are heavily regulated may have higher barriers to entry for new firms and more established firms with the resources to comply with regulatory requirements. In contrast, industries with lower levels of regulation may be more accessible to new entrants.

Understanding industry structure is important for firms as they seek to develop strategies to compete effectively within their industry. By analyzing the competitive landscape, firms can identify opportunities to differentiate their offerings, reduce costs, or seek out new markets. Similarly, policymakers and regulators can use an understanding of industry structure to develop policies that promote competition, innovation, and consumer welfare.

THE COMPETITIVE FORCES IN INDUSTRY STRUCTURE

The concept of industry structure is essential in understanding the competitive forces that influence firms' strategic decision-making. The competitive forces are the sources of competition within an industry and include the threat of new entrants, bargaining power of suppliers, bargaining power of buyers, threat of substitute products or services, and rivalry among existing competitors. These forces create an environment where firms must compete to gain and maintain market share.

1. **Threat of New Entrants:** The ease with which new firms can enter an industry is a critical determinant of the intensity of competition within the industry. If barriers to entry are low, new entrants can quickly and easily enter the market, intensifying competition and reducing the profitability of existing firms. Barriers to entry can include economies of scale, product differentiation, capital requirements, government regulations, and access to distribution channels.

Existing firms can deter new entrants by creating barriers to entry, such as through patent protection, brand loyalty, and economies of scale. The threat of new entrants is highest in industries where there are low barriers to entry and firms are not protected by strong intellectual property rights or government regulations.

2. **Bargaining Power of Suppliers:** Suppliers can exert power over firms by controlling the quality and availability of key inputs, increasing their prices, or imposing unfavorable terms. Suppliers can also exert power if there are a limited number of suppliers and if the cost of switching suppliers is high. In industries with high supplier power, firms are less often able to negotiate favorable prices or terms, reducing their profitability.

3. **Bargaining Power of Buyers:** Buyers can exert power over firms by demanding lower prices, better quality, or more favorable terms. They can also exert power if they can switch easily to alternative suppliers or purchase in large volumes. In industries with high buyer power, firms may be forced to lower prices or offer better terms, reducing their profitability.

4. **Threat of Substitute Products or Services:** Substitute products or services are those that can replace or compete with the products or services offered by firms in an industry. The threat of substitutes is highest in industries with many close substitutes available and switching costs are low. Firms in industries facing a high threat of substitutes must continually innovate to differentiate their products or services and maintain their market position.

5. **Rivalry Among Existing Competitors:** The intensity of rivalry among existing competitors is a function of the number of competitors, their relative size and power, and the industry growth rate. Rivalry is highest in industries with many competitors, low levels of product differentiation, and slow industry growth. Firms in highly competitive industries must continually invest in product differentiation and cost-cutting to maintain profitability.

To summarize, industry structure refers to the competitive environment within which firms operate, and the five competitive forces are threat of new entrants, bargaining power of suppliers, bargaining power of buyers, threat of substitute products or services, and rivalry among existing competitors. Understanding these forces is critical to developing a competitive strategy that enables firms to compete effectively and maintain their market position.

HOW TO EVALUATE AN INDUSTRY STRUCTURE USING PORTER'S FIVE FORCES MODEL

Previously, we briefly discussed Porter's Five Forces model and the fact that it is a framework used to evaluate the structure of an industry. This model provides a systematic approach to analyzing the competitive forces that shape an industry and can help businesses make informed decisions about how to position themselves within that industry.

The five forces identified in Porter's model are the threat of new entrants, the bargaining power of suppliers, the bargaining power of buyers, the threat of substitute products or services, and the intensity of rivalry among existing competitors. These forces interact with each other to determine the overall level of competition in the industry.

To evaluate an industry structure using Porter's Five Forces model, businesses must first assess the strength of each of the five forces. This involves analyzing factors such as the size of the market, the level of competition, the availability of substitutes, the power of suppliers and buyers, and the ease of entry into the market. By doing this, businesses can determine which forces are the strongest and which are the weakest and decide how to respond to those forces.

For example, if the threat of new entrants is high, businesses may need to focus on building brand awareness and developing customer loyalty to create a barrier to entry. They may also need to invest in research and development to stay ahead of potential new competitors.

If the bargaining power of suppliers is high, businesses may need to develop closer relationships with their suppliers or even consider vertical integration to reduce their dependence on outside suppliers.

If the bargaining power of buyers is high, businesses may need to offer competitive pricing or improve the quality of their products or services to attract and retain customers.

If the threat of substitute products or services is high, businesses may need to focus on developing unique products or services that cannot be easily substituted. Alternatively, they may need to consider entering into partnerships or alliances with other businesses to gain a competitive edge.

If the rivalry among existing competitors is high, businesses may need to focus on building their brand, expanding their product or service offerings, or cutting costs to remain competitive.

In conclusion, evaluating industry structure using Porter's Five Forces model is a valuable tool for businesses looking to make strategic decisions about positioning themselves in the marketplace. By analyzing the strength of each of the five forces, businesses can better understand the competitive dynamics of their industry and make informed decisions about how to respond to those forces.

THE IMPLICATIONS FOR ENTREPRENEURS IN EACH INDUSTRY STRUCTURE

The implications for entrepreneurship in each industry structure are unique and vary depending on the competitive forces present in the industry. Here are some possible implications for entrepreneurship in each industry structure:

- **Perfect Competition:** In a perfectly competitive market, entrepreneurship can be challenging as there are no significant barriers to entry. The market is saturated, and it can be challenging to differentiate a product or service from existing competitors. New entrepreneurs must find a unique value proposition and offer superior customer service or lower prices to gain a foothold in the market. This market structure may favor entrepreneurs with low-cost structures, as they can compete on price.

- **Monopolistic Competition:** In a monopolistically competitive market, entrepreneurs may have a better chance of success because there is some differentiation among competitors. The key to success in this market is to develop a unique value proposition and a strong brand identity that sets your product or service apart from others. Entrepreneurs must be able to create a positive perception of their brand in the minds of consumers.

- **Oligopoly:** In an oligopolistic market, entrepreneurs may face significant barriers to entry due to the dominance of a few large players in the market. These firms often have established brands, economies of scale, and significant financial resources. New entrants may find it difficult to compete on price, but they may be able to offer new and innovative products or services that appeal to a niche market. However, entrepreneurs must be prepared to face intense competition from established firms that may attempt to copy their products or services.

- **Monopoly:** In a monopoly, entrepreneurship is limited as there is only one dominant player in the market. However, entrepreneurs may still be able to identify niches within the market that are not being served and offer new and innovative products or services. The key to monopoly success is to offer a unique value proposition that cannot be found elsewhere.

- **Competitive Markets:** In a competitive market, entrepreneurs face a mix of opportunities and challenges. The presence of numerous competitors can make it difficult to gain market share, but it also creates a range of potential customers. The key to success in this market is to develop a unique value proposition and create a strong brand identity. Entrepreneurs must be able to differentiate their product or service from competitors and offer something not currently available.

Overall, entrepreneurship can be challenging in any market structure, but each has opportunities. The key is to identify the unique characteristics of the market and develop a strategy that leverages the competitive forces present in the industry. Successful entrepreneurs must be innovative, creative, and willing to take risks to achieve success.

TIMING AND WINDOWS OF OPPORTUNITY

Timing and windows of opportunity are critical factors in the success of entrepreneurship. A window of opportunity is a period of time during which a specific opportunity exists and can be exploited. Identifying the right time to enter the market can be just as important as having a great business idea. Entrepreneurs who enter the market at the right time can gain a competitive advantage, whereas those who enter too early or too late may struggle to succeed.

Timing is crucial in the development of new products or services, as well as in entering new markets. The timing of market entry can significantly impact a business's success. Entering a market too early can result in the business spending too much money on marketing and product development, only to find that consumers are not ready for the product or service. Entering a market too late can result in the business being crowded out by established competitors who have already captured the market share. Therefore, the right timing of market entry is crucial.

In some cases, specific windows of opportunity exist for entrepreneurs. These windows of opportunity may be driven by factors such as changes in technology, consumer preferences, or economic conditions. Entrepreneurs who can identify these windows of opportunity can exploit them to gain a competitive advantage. However, these windows of opportunity are often short-lived, and entrepreneurs must act quickly to take advantage of them.

Entrepreneurs must also be aware of the timing of their own personal circumstances when launching a new venture. For example, an entrepreneur still in school or with significant personal commitments may struggle to devote enough time and resources to the business. Similarly, entrepreneurs who are too risk-averse or lack the necessary skills and experience may struggle to launch a successful venture.

In conclusion, timing and windows of opportunity are critical factors in the success of entrepreneurship. Entrepreneurs who are able to identify the right time to enter the market and exploit specific windows of opportunity can gain a competitive advantage. However, market entry timing can be difficult to predict, and entrepreneurs must be prepared to adapt to changing market conditions. Additionally, entrepreneurs must also be aware of the timing of their own personal circumstances when launching a new venture.

ENTRY STRATEGIES FOR DIFFERENT STAGES OF INDUSTRY LIFECYCLE

The strategy for entering a particular stage of the industry lifecycle varies depending on the industry and the entrepreneur's goals. Here are some common entry strategies for each stage of the industry lifecycle:

1. **Introduction:** The entry strategy for this stage involves developing a new product or service that meets an unmet customer need. Entrepreneurs should focus on gaining market share and building brand awareness through aggressive marketing campaigns. This could include offering free trials, product demonstrations, or pricing discounts to attract early adopters. A key consideration is the entry timing, as entering too early could lead to significant costs without generating sufficient revenue.

2. **Growth:** At this stage, the focus is on expanding the customer base and building a competitive advantage. Entrepreneurs may consider offering new products or services, entering new geographic markets, or seeking strategic partnerships or acquisitions. This could involve investing in research and development to drive innovation or implementing cost-cutting measures to increase profitability.

3. **Maturity:** In this stage, the market becomes saturated, and demand for existing products or services slows down. Entrepreneurs should focus on optimizing operations and reducing costs to maintain profitability. They may also need to explore new product or service offerings or consider merging with or acquiring other companies to gain a competitive edge. A key strategy for success at this stage is differentiating products or services from competitors to maintain market share.

4. **Decline:** The entry strategy for this stage involves identifying declining industries and seeking opportunities for repositioning or innovation. Entrepreneurs may consider developing substitute products or services, entering new markets, or seeking to acquire existing firms at a lower price. They may also need to consider exiting the industry altogether if the market becomes unprofitable.

In addition, entrepreneurs must consider the timing of their entry into the industry. Early entry into a new market can allow entrepreneurs to establish themselves as industry leaders and gain a competitive advantage. However, early entry also comes with significant risk and uncertainty, including high costs and unknown customer demand. A late entry into a mature industry may mean fewer opportunities for growth, but it also comes with lower costs and established demand. Therefore, entry timing is an important consideration when evaluating entry strategies.

TECHNIQUES TO IDENTIFY UNTAPPED OPPORTUNITIES IN COMPETITIVE INDUSTRIES

Identifying untapped opportunities in competitive industries can be a challenging task, but it is crucial for entrepreneurs to succeed. Here are some techniques to help identify such opportunities:

- **Market Research:** Conducting in-depth market research is crucial to identify untapped opportunities. This includes gathering information on the market size, consumer behavior, competitors, and trends shaping the industry. This information can help entrepreneurs understand market gaps and identify potential growth areas.
- **Customer Feedback:** Gathering feedback from customers can provide valuable insights into their needs and preferences. Entrepreneurs can use this feedback to identify areas where existing products or services are falling short or where new products or services may be needed.

- **Industry Trends:** Keeping up with industry trends can help entrepreneurs identify new opportunities. By staying current on technological advancements, social and cultural changes, and other trends, entrepreneurs can anticipate new needs and identify areas where they can offer innovative solutions.

- **Partnering with Other Companies:** Collaborating with other companies, especially those that complement their offerings, can be a great way to identify untapped opportunities. Entrepreneurs can leverage the strengths of their partners to expand their offerings or reach new markets.

- **Niche Markets:** Targeting niche markets that are underserved or overlooked by larger competitors can be a great way to identify untapped opportunities. By offering specialized products or services that meet the unique needs of a particular group of consumers, entrepreneurs can gain a competitive advantage and build a loyal customer base.

- **Disruptive Innovation:** Disruptive innovation involves introducing a new product or service that fundamentally changes the industry. Entrepreneurs can identify untapped opportunities by looking for areas where existing products or services can be improved or replaced by something entirely new.

In summary, identifying untapped opportunities in competitive industries requires entrepreneurs to be proactive in researching the market, gathering customer feedback, keeping up with industry trends, collaborating with others, targeting niche markets, and being open to disruptive innovations. By doing so, entrepreneurs can gain a competitive advantage and create successful businesses in even the most competitive industries.

How Agile Companies Adapt to Changes in Industry Structure

Agile companies can adapt to changes in industry structure by being flexible and responsive to changes in the competitive environment. They are able to identify new opportunities and take advantage of them quickly while also being able to respond to threats in the market. There are several strategies that agile companies use to adapt to changes in industry structure.

One strategy is to constantly monitor changes in the competitive landscape. This can involve keeping track of competitors, suppliers, customers, and new entrants in the market. Companies can use market research and analysis to gather data on these factors, which can then be used to identify trends and opportunities.

Another strategy is to invest in innovation and research and development. This can involve developing new products or services, improving existing products or services, or finding new ways to deliver value to customers. Agile companies can often respond to changes in the market by quickly developing and launching new products or services that meet customer needs.

Agile companies also tend to have a strong focus on customer experience. They are able to respond quickly to customer feedback and adapt their products and services to meet changing customer needs. This can involve gathering feedback through surveys, focus groups, or other means and using that feedback to inform product development and marketing strategies.

In addition, agile companies tend to have a culture of experimentation and risk-taking. They are willing to try new things and take risks, even if they might not always succeed. This allows them to quickly test and iterate on new ideas, and to respond quickly to changes in the market.

Finally, agile companies tend to be highly collaborative and cross-functional. They can break down silos and work together across different departments and functions to quickly respond to changes in the market. This can involve cross-functional teams working on specific projects or the use of agile methodologies to facilitate collaboration and communication across different teams and departments.

In summary, agile companies are able to adapt to changes in industry structure by constantly monitoring the market, investing in innovation and R&D, focusing on customer experience, fostering a culture of experimentation and risk-taking, and promoting collaboration and cross-functional teamwork.

EXPLORING THE RIDE-HAILING INDUSTRY FROM THE PERSPECTIVE OF UBER

The ride-hailing industry is a relatively new segment of the transportation industry that utilizes technology to connect riders with drivers. This industry has seen significant growth in recent years due to the convenience, accessibility, and low cost compared to traditional taxis. One of the most well-known and successful companies in this industry is Uber.

Travis Kalanick and Garrett Camp started the company with the goal of making it easier for people to get around cities. The idea was simple: Create an app that connects people who need a ride with drivers who can give them one. The app would allow customers to track the location of their ride and make payments electronically, making the entire experience more convenient.

Uber's entry into the industry was disruptive, as it challenged the traditional taxi industry's business model. Unlike taxi companies, Uber drivers were not required to obtain commercial licenses, undergo rigorous background checks, or follow strict fare regulations. The Uber app also allowed drivers to work on their own schedule and set their own rates, leading to greater flexibility and earning potential. Additionally, Uber's pricing model was based on demand, meaning that prices would go up during peak hours or in areas with high demand. This controversial dynamic pricing model led to accusations of price gouging, especially during emergencies or natural disasters.

Despite initial pushback from traditional taxi companies and regulatory agencies, Uber's entry into the ride-hailing industry was successful. The company quickly expanded to other cities in the United States and then to other countries around the world. The company also introduced other services like UberX, which allowed drivers to use their own personal cars for rides, and Uber POOL, which enables passengers to share a ride and split the cost.

Uber faced numerous challenges, including regulatory hurdles, safety concerns, and public relations issues related to its treatment of drivers and workplace culture. Despite these challenges, Uber remains one of the dominant players in the ride-hailing industry.

The ride-hailing industry is currently in the growth stage of the industry lifecycle, with Uber being one of the largest players in the market. The industry is highly competitive, with low barriers to entry, and intense competition among players. Uber's business model has enabled it to scale rapidly and expand into new markets, but the company has also faced significant challenges related to regulation, legal battles, and reputational damage. As the industry continues to evolve, it will be interesting to see how Uber and other players in the market adapt to the changing industry structure and maintain their competitive edge.

Uber's success results from several factors, including its innovative approach to the ride-hailing industry, its use of technology, and its ability to adapt to changes in industry structure and lifecycle.

First, Uber was able to identify and capitalize on a window of opportunity in the ride-hailing industry. By entering the market during the growth stage of the industry lifecycle, Uber established itself as a dominant player in the industry. This allowed the company to achieve economies of scale and create a network effect that made it difficult for new entrants to compete.

Second, Uber's success is also due to its innovative use of technology. The company's platform, which connects drivers with riders, is based on a mobile app that is easy to use and highly intuitive. This allowed Uber to create a differentiated product offering that differentiates it from traditional taxi services. The platform also allows for real-time tracking of drivers, automated payment processing, and personalized user experiences, further enhancing the customer experience.

Finally, Uber's ability to adapt to industry structure and lifecycle changes has also contributed to its success. As the industry has matured and become more competitive, Uber has expanded into new markets and diversified its product offering. This includes the introduction of UberEATS, a food delivery service, and Uber POOL, a carpooling service. By diversifying its product offering, Uber has continued to grow and maintain its market share.

In addition to these factors, Uber's success is due to its ability to manage costs and optimize its operations. The company has implemented a range of cost-cutting measures, including the use of dynamic pricing, which allows it to adjust its pricing in real-time based on demand. Uber has also implemented a range of operational efficiencies, such as driver incentives and flexible working arrangements, which have helped to reduce its costs while improving its service offering.

Overall, Uber's success results from a combination of factors, including its innovative approach to the ride-hailing industry, its use of technology, and its ability to adapt to changes in industry structure and lifecycle. By continuing to innovate and diversify its product offering while focusing on cost management and operational efficiency, Uber is well-positioned to continue to be a dominant player in the ride-hailing industry.

THE IMPORTANCE OF UNDERSTANDING INDUSTRY STATUS FOR ENTREPRENEURIAL SUCCESS

Understanding the status of an industry is crucial for entrepreneurial success. It allows entrepreneurs to identify opportunities and challenges in the industry as well as the right time and entry strategy for their venture. Industry status can refer to the current stage of the industry lifecycle and the prevailing industry structure and competitive forces.

For example, an entrepreneur who understands the industry lifecycle can identify opportunities and challenges associated with each stage. In the early stages of the lifecycle, entrepreneurs can enter a growing market with innovative products or services, while in the later stages, they may need to focus on cost-cutting and operational efficiency. This knowledge can inform an entrepreneur's business plan and help them to better position their venture for success.

Similarly, understanding the prevailing industry structure and competitive forces can help entrepreneurs identify the barriers to entry and determine the best entry strategy. For example, a highly concentrated industry dominated by a few large players may require a different approach than a fragmented industry with many small players. An entrepreneur who understands the bargaining power of suppliers and buyers and the threat of new entrants and substitute products can develop strategies to mitigate those risks and create a sustainable competitive advantage.

Furthermore, understanding the industry status allows entrepreneurs to stay ahead of the competition and anticipate future changes in the market. By monitoring industry trends and changes, entrepreneurs can identify new opportunities and threats and adjust their strategy accordingly. This knowledge can influence an entrepreneur's decision-making and help them better allocate resources and make strategic investments.

In conclusion, understanding the status of an industry is crucial for entrepreneurial success. It enables entrepreneurs to identify opportunities and challenges, determine the right entry time and strategy, and stay ahead of the competition. By monitoring industry trends and changes, entrepreneurs can make informed decisions that will position their venture for success in the long run.

Summary

In summary, understanding industry lifecycle and industry structure is crucial for entrepreneurship as they provide insights into the dynamics and characteristics of the industry, helping entrepreneurs identify opportunities and challenges and influencing strategic decision-making. Industry lifecycle describes the stages of growth, maturity, decline, and potential rebirth of an industry, while industry structure refers to the competitive forces and market conditions within an industry, including the threat of new entrants, bargaining power of suppliers and buyers, the threat of substitutes, and intensity of rivalry among competitors.

Entrepreneurs can use industry lifecycle and structure analysis to evaluate the potential of an industry for new entry, identify opportunities and threats, assess the competitive landscape, and develop effective strategies for long-term success. In the early stages of an industry, entrepreneurship is characterized by high risk and high reward, with potential for high growth and innovation. However, as industries mature, opportunities for entrepreneurship may shift towards improving efficiency, cost-cutting, and differentiation in the face of intense competition.

Successful entrepreneurship requires agility and adaptability to changing industry dynamics, as seen in the case of Uber. Uber disrupted the taxi industry by using technology to provide a more convenient and cost-effective service to consumers, taking advantage of the changing dynamics of the transportation industry. However, the company faced regulatory and legal challenges as the industry structure changed and had to adapt by developing new strategies to compete with established players and survive in the mature stage of the industry lifecycle.

Overall, entrepreneurship success requires a deep understanding of industry dynamics, including industry lifecycle and structure, and the ability to identify opportunities and adapt to changing conditions. Entrepreneurs who can navigate the complexities of industry dynamics are better equipped to achieve long-term success and make a lasting impact in their respective industries.

12. Macroeconomic Change

Luck is what happens when preparation meets opportunity.

Seneca

Roman Philosopher

Macroeconomics deals with the performance of a large economy and its vast number of influencing factors. For entrepreneurs, it's valuable to understand how the needs and wants of your target audience are influenced by the world around them.

This chapter explores this complex world, emphasizing *demographic* and *psychographic* changes. Changes in *technology, society, politics,* and *regulations* are also examined, as these are central to entrepreneurs' understanding of their customers' buying behaviors.

The Opportunity Analysis Canvas

Emphasis on "Macroeconomic Change"

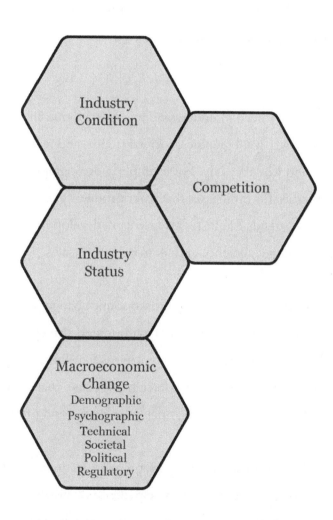

Understanding macroeconomic change is crucial for entrepreneurs because it helps them identify potential opportunities and threats in the business environment. Macroeconomic changes refer to the broad changes that occur in the economy and affect the behavior of consumers, businesses, and the overall market. These changes can significantly impact a business' success, and entrepreneurs who stay informed about macroeconomic trends are better equipped to make informed decisions and respond to changes in the market.

One of the key reasons entrepreneurs need to understand macroeconomic change is that it affects consumer behavior. Changes in demographics, psychographics, societal trends, and technology can influence what consumers buy, how they buy, and why they buy. For example, a demographic shift towards an aging population may create opportunities for businesses that offer products and services catering to the needs of older people. Understanding these trends can help entrepreneurs develop marketing and advertising strategies that resonate with their target audience and ultimately drive sales.

Another reason entrepreneurs need to understand macroeconomic change is that it affects the availability of resources and costs. Changes in political and regulatory environments can create new opportunities or pose challenges for entrepreneurs. For instance, changes in regulations may impact the availability of funding, access to technology, or the cost of raw materials. Understanding these changes can help entrepreneurs make better decisions on the allocation of resources, pricing strategies, and product development.

In summary, macroeconomic changes are critical for entrepreneurs to understand, as they provide insights into the current and future state of the market and can help identify new opportunities and threats. Entrepreneurs who stay informed about macroeconomic trends and adapt their strategies accordingly are better positioned for long-term success.

THE ELEMENTS OF MACROECONOMIC CHANGE

Understanding macroeconomic change is essential for entrepreneurs as it enables them to identify the trends that shape customer preferences, anticipate future needs, and identify potential opportunities for innovation.

The following are the key elements of macroeconomic change that entrepreneurs need to understand:

- **Demographic Changes**: Demographic changes refer to shifts in the composition of populations. Changes in age, ethnicity, gender, and income can impact consumer behavior, as they influence how people spend their money, what they buy, and how they shop. For example, an aging population may have different needs and preferences than a younger population.

- **Psychographic Changes**: Psychographic changes refer to shifts in consumer attitudes, values, and beliefs. As society evolves, people's attitudes toward issues such as social responsibility, sustainability, and health can change. Entrepreneurs need to be aware of these changes, as they can impact how consumers perceive their products and services.

- **Technological Changes**: Technological changes refer to advances in technology that impact the way people work, live, and interact. Technological innovations can create new markets, disrupt existing ones, and change the way people consume products and services. Entrepreneurs must be aware of new technologies and their potential to impact their industry, as they may need to adapt their business models to stay competitive.

- **Societal Changes**: Societal changes refer to shifts in social norms, lifestyles, and culture. For example, changing attitudes towards health and wellness may drive demand for healthy food and fitness products. Entrepreneurs need to be aware of these changes and their impact on consumer behavior.

- **Political Changes**: Political changes refer to changes in government policies, regulations, and laws. These changes can impact business costs, create new opportunities, and change the competitive landscape. Entrepreneurs need to be aware of these changes and their potential impact on their industry.

- **Regulatory Changes**: Regulatory changes refer to changes in laws and regulations that impact business operations. For example, environmental regulation changes may impact the way companies manufacture and distribute their products. Entrepreneurs need to be aware of regulatory changes and their potential impact on their industry, as they may need to adapt their business models to comply with new regulations.

By understanding these elements of macroeconomic change, entrepreneurs can better anticipate their target audience's changing needs and preferences and identify opportunities for innovation.

Demographic Changes

Demographic changes refer to shifts in the characteristics of a population, including factors such as age, gender, ethnicity, income, and education. These changes can significantly impact entrepreneurship because they influence consumer behavior, market demand, and business opportunities.

For example, the aging of the population can create new business opportunities in industries such as healthcare and senior care, as there is an increasing demand for products and services that cater to the needs of older individuals. Similarly, changes in the ethnic composition of the population can create opportunities for entrepreneurs who specialize in catering to the cultural preferences and needs of specific communities.

Changes in demographics can also impact the workforce, which can have implications for entrepreneurship. For example, an increase in the number of women in the workforce can create new opportunities for businesses catering to working mothers' needs, such as childcare services or flexible work arrangements.

Entrepreneurs need to be aware of demographic changes and their implications for their business. This involves understanding the characteristics and needs of their target audience and identifying emerging trends and shifts in the population. By staying attuned to demographic changes, entrepreneurs can identify new business opportunities and adapt their strategies to changing market demand.

AN ANALYSIS OF CURRENT DEMOGRAPHIC TRENDS IN THE U.S.

The demographic landscape of the United States is constantly changing, driven by factors such as changing birth and death rates, immigration patterns, and shifting cultural norms. Some of the most notable demographic trends in the U.S. include an aging population, increasing diversity, and changing family structures.

The aging U.S. population is a major demographic trend that is heavily influencing various aspects of society, including healthcare, retirement, and the labor force. According to the U.S. Census Bureau, by 2030, all baby boomers will be older than 65 years old, and there will be more Americans over 65 than under 18 for the first time in U.S. history. This shift is expected to place significant strains on government resources such as Social Security, Medicare, and businesses that rely on an active and productive workforce.

Another significant demographic trend in the U.S. is increasing diversity, particularly with respect to race and ethnicity. The U.S. Census Bureau projects that the country will become "majority-minority" by 2045, meaning that non-Hispanic whites will comprise less than 50% of the population. This shift is driven largely by increases in the Hispanic and Asian populations and has important implications for entrepreneurs in terms of marketing, product development, and workforce diversity.

Changing family structures is another key demographic trend in the U.S., driven in part by declining marriage rates and increasing numbers of single-parent households. According to the Pew Research Center, in 2019, only about half of adults in the U.S. were married, down from 72% in 1960. This trend has important implications for entrepreneurs in terms of understanding the needs and preferences of different household types and how these changes may impact consumer spending patterns.

Overall, these demographic trends and others are critical for entrepreneurs to understand, as they can have significant impacts on market demand, labor force availability, and consumer preferences. By staying informed and adapting to these changes, entrepreneurs can position themselves to capitalize on new opportunities and succeed in a rapidly evolving marketplace.

Differences in Consumer Behavior Across Different Age Groups and Ethnicities

Consumer behavior can differ significantly based on age group and ethnicity in the U.S. Understanding these differences is critical for entrepreneurs looking to target specific customer segments and create effective marketing strategies.

Age is a significant factor in consumer behavior. Younger generations, such as Gen Z and Millennials, tend to be more tech-savvy and value experiences and social responsibility in their purchasing decisions. In contrast, older generations, such as Baby Boomers and the Silent Generation, may prioritize brand loyalty and practicality.

Ethnicity can also impact consumer behavior, with different ethnic groups often having unique cultural values and preferences. For example, Hispanic consumers tend to prioritize family, tradition, and community in their purchasing decisions, while Asian Americans tend to value education and financial stability. African American consumers may place a higher emphasis on the authenticity and cultural relevance of products and brands.

It's worth noting that consumer behavior is not solely defined by age or ethnicity, as individual preferences and circumstances also play a significant role. However, understanding these demographic trends can provide entrepreneurs with valuable insights into the needs and wants of their target audiences and help them tailor their products, services, and marketing efforts accordingly.

Psychographic Changes

Psychographic changes are changes in consumer behavior and lifestyle that are related to their personality, values, attitudes, and interests. These changes are driven by numerous factors, such as advancements in technology, changes in social norms, and shifting economic conditions. Psychographic changes heavily impact entrepreneurship because they influence consumer behavior and purchasing decisions. Entrepreneurs who understand these changes can tailor their products and services to meet the evolving needs and preferences of their target market.

One example of a psychographic change is the growing demand for sustainable and environmentally friendly products. As consumers become more environmentally conscious, they are more likely to seek out products that align with their values. Entrepreneurs who recognize this trend can create more eco-friendly products and market them to consumers who value sustainability.

Another example of a psychographic change is the trend toward health and wellness. As consumers become more focused on their health, they are more likely to seek products promoting wellness and fitness. Entrepreneurs who recognize this trend can create products that are tailored to this market, such as healthy food and beverages, fitness equipment, or health and wellness apps.

Psychographic changes can also be related to changing social norms and values. For example, there has been a growing awareness of mental health issues, which has led to an increased demand for products and services that support mental well-being. Entrepreneurs who recognize this trend can create products designed to help consumers manage stress and improve their mental health.

In summary, psychographic changes reflect changes in consumer behavior that are driven by evolving values, attitudes, and interests. Understanding these changes is important for entrepreneurs because it enables them to create products and services that meet their target market's evolving needs and preferences. By staying attuned to psychographic changes, entrepreneurs can identify opportunities to innovate and create products that are tailored to the changing needs of consumers.

An Analysis of Current Psychographic Trends in the U.S.

Psychographic trends are changes in people's attitudes, values, beliefs, and lifestyles that affect consumer behavior. These changes are significant for entrepreneurs because they affect the way people perceive and use products and services. In the US, some current psychographic trends include a growing focus on health and wellness, increased interest in sustainability, and a greater emphasis on convenience and efficiency.

The focus on health and wellness has become a major trend in recent years, with more people becoming interested in healthy eating, exercise, and overall wellness. This trend has led to a surge in demand for organic and natural foods, gym memberships, and other health and wellness products and services. For entrepreneurs, this trend presents an opportunity to create new products and services that cater to this growing demand.

Sustainability is another psychographic trend that has gained traction in recent years. Consumers are becoming more aware of the impact of their actions on the environment and are actively seeking out products and services that are sustainable and eco-friendly. This trend has led to a rise in sustainable products, from eco-friendly cleaning products to electric cars. Entrepreneurs who are able to incorporate sustainability into their business models may be able to tap into this growing demand.

Convenience and efficiency are also key psychographic trends that are shaping consumer behavior. People today lead busy lives and are often short on time, which has led to a growing demand for products and services that are convenient and efficient. This trend has led to the rise of on-demand services, from ridesharing to meal delivery, that cater to people's desire for quick and easy access to products and services. Entrepreneurs who are able to offer convenient and efficient solutions may be able to capture a share of this market.

In summary, current psychographic trends in the US include a growing focus on health and wellness, increased interest in sustainability, and a greater emphasis on convenience and efficiency. Entrepreneurs who can tap into these trends may be able to create successful businesses that cater to the changing needs and wants of consumers.

DIFFERENCES IN CONSUMER VALUES AND BELIEFS AND HOW THEY IMPACT BUYING BEHAVIOR

Consumer values and beliefs are deeply ingrained in an individual's psyche, shaping their attitudes and behaviors towards various products and services. As such, understanding these values and beliefs is essential for entrepreneurs seeking to create and market products that will resonate with their target audience.

One important consumer value in the U.S. is individualism, which emphasizes personal freedom and self-expression. This value encourages consumers to make purchases that reflect their individual tastes and values, leading to a high demand for customized and personalized products. On the other hand, collectivism, which emphasizes group harmony and interdependence, is also prevalent in some communities, particularly among Asian Americans and Hispanic Americans.

Another important consumer value is the emphasis on health and wellness, with a growing trend towards natural and organic products. Concerns over the impact of environmental pollutants and the use of chemicals in food and personal care products have fueled this trend. The trend towards sustainability is also growing, with consumers becoming more aware of the impact of their purchasing decisions on the environment and society.

Overall, entrepreneurs who can effectively understand and cater to the values and beliefs of their target audience will have a greater chance of success in the marketplace. By aligning their products and messaging with these values, they can create a deeper connection with their customers, leading to increased brand loyalty and a higher likelihood of repeat purchases.

Technological Changes

Technological changes refer to technological advances that impact the products, services, and processes of a given industry. Technological changes can enable the creation of new products, improve efficiency and quality, and disrupt existing business models. For entrepreneurs, technological changes present both opportunities and challenges.

One way technological changes impact entrepreneurship is by creating new markets for innovative products and services. Entrepreneurs can take advantage of emerging technologies to create new business models and services that address unmet needs. This can lead to the creation of new industries, such as ridesharing, mobile payments, and cloud computing. In addition, technological changes can also improve existing products and services, enabling entrepreneurs to differentiate themselves from their competitors and attract new customers.

However, technological changes can also pose significant challenges for entrepreneurs. Disruptive technologies, such as the internet and smartphones, can fundamentally alter the way industries operate, making existing business models obsolete. Entrepreneurs who fail to adapt to new technologies risk being left behind, losing market share, and ultimately failing.

Technological changes can also impact the nature of work and the skills required of employees. For example, automation and artificial intelligence can replace human workers in certain tasks, leading to the need for new skills and training. Entrepreneurs who adapt to these changes and invest in the necessary technology and training can gain a competitive advantage.

Overall, technological changes have a significant impact on entrepreneurship, creating both opportunities and challenges. Entrepreneurs who can stay abreast of emerging technologies, and adapt their products, services, and business models to changing market demands, are more likely to succeed.

UNDERSTANDING TECHNOLOGY ADOPTION RATES AND THE IMPACT OF EMERGING TECHNOLOGIES ON CONSUMER BEHAVIOR

Technology adoption rate refers to the speed at which new technology is embraced by consumers. The rate of adoption is influenced by factors such as the cost of the technology, the perceived benefits of the technology, and the level of technological literacy in the population.

Emerging technologies, such as artificial intelligence, the Internet of Things, and blockchain, are having a significant impact on consumer behavior in the U.S. These technologies are changing the way consumers shop, interact with businesses, and make purchase decisions. For example, the rise of e-commerce platforms and the use of mobile devices for shopping have made it easier for consumers to compare prices and access a wide range of products. This has led to increased price sensitivity and reduced brand loyalty.

Artificial intelligence (AI) is another emerging technology that is transforming the way businesses interact with consumers. AI-powered chatbots are increasingly being used to provide customer service, answer questions, and handle complaints. This has reduced the need for human customer service representatives and has made it possible for businesses to provide 24/7 customer support.

The Internet of Things (IoT) is also having a significant impact on consumer behavior. The IoT refers to the network of devices that are connected to the internet and can communicate with each other. Smart home devices, such as thermostats, security systems, and lighting, are becoming increasingly popular. These devices are making it possible for consumers to control their homes remotely, which is leading to increased convenience and energy savings.

Finally, blockchain technology is changing the way consumers make purchase decisions. Blockchain is a decentralized, secure ledger that can be used to track transactions. This technology is being used to create digital currencies, such as Bitcoin, which can be used to make purchases. This has the potential to reduce transaction costs and increase security.

In conclusion, emerging technologies are having a significant impact on consumer behavior in the U.S. Entrepreneurs who understand these trends and can leverage these technologies to create innovative products and services will be well-positioned to succeed in the marketplace.

Societal Changes

Societal changes refer to the transformation of social structures, values, attitudes, and behaviors of people in a society. These changes can be triggered by various factors such as demographic changes, economic development, technological advancements, and cultural shifts. In the context of entrepreneurship, societal changes can heavily influence the needs and wants of customers, the competitive landscape, and the overall business environment. Entrepreneurs who can identify and adapt to these changes can gain a competitive advantage and achieve long-term success.

One example of societal change is the growing emphasis on work-life balance. With advances in technology, more people are able to work remotely or set their own schedules. This has led to a demand for products and services that cater to individuals who prioritize their personal lives over their work lives. It has also led to the rise of companies that offer flexible work arrangements, telecommuting options, and time-saving services such as meal delivery and cleaning services.

Overall, societal changes can have a profound impact on the entrepreneurial landscape. By staying abreast of these changes, entrepreneurs can develop innovative solutions that meet the evolving needs of their customers and create new business opportunities.

An Analysis of Current Societal Trends in the U.S.

First, there is a growing emphasis on health and wellness. Consumers are becoming more health-conscious and seeking products and services that promote their physical and mental well-being. This trend has led to the rise of the fitness and wellness industry, including companies offering organic and healthy food options, gyms, and mental health services.

Second, there is a growing focus on sustainability and social responsibility. Consumers are becoming more aware of their impact on the environment and society and are seeking companies that prioritize sustainability and ethical business practices. This has produced the green economy, which is comprised of companies offering eco-friendly products, renewable energy, and sustainable manufacturing processes.

Third, there is a growing emphasis on diversity and inclusion. Consumers are seeking out companies that prioritize diversity and inclusion and are becoming more conscious of the representation of underrepresented groups in media and marketing. This has resulted in more companies that prioritize diversity and inclusion, including those that offer products and services for underrepresented communities.

Finally, there is a growing trend toward convenience and automation. Consumers are seeking out products and services that offer convenience and automation, from online shopping and meal delivery to home automation systems. This has promoted the rise of companies that offer on-demand services and technologies that make consumers' lives easier and more efficient.

These societal trends have significant implications for entrepreneurship in the U.S. Companies that identify and respond to these trends are more likely to succeed because they are able to meet the evolving needs and desires of consumers. Additionally, companies that prioritize sustainability, diversity, and inclusion are more likely to build strong relationships with consumers and gain their loyalty over the long term. Finally, companies that prioritize convenience and automation are more likely to thrive in a fast-paced, on-demand economy.

UNDERSTANDING THE CULTURAL AND SOCIAL CHANGES THAT IMPACT CONSUMER BEHAVIOR IN THE U.S.

Consumer behavior is influenced by various cultural and social factors in the United States. These factors shape consumers' perceptions, attitudes, and beliefs about products and services. Understanding these changes is important for entrepreneurs as they develop products and services that resonate with their target audience. Some of the cultural and social changes that impact consumer behavior in the U.S. include the following:

- **Diversity and Inclusion:** The U.S. is becoming increasingly diverse, with people from different ethnicities, cultures, and religions living together. This diversity has led to a growing demand for products and services that cater to the needs of different cultural groups.

- **Changing Family Structures:** Family structures are changing in the U.S. with more people opting for non-traditional family arrangements, such as single-parent households, blended families, and same-sex households. This shift is changing the way consumers purchase products and services.

- **Health and Wellness:** Consumers are becoming more health-conscious and focused on wellness. There is a growing demand for products and services that promote a healthy lifestyle, including organic foods, exercise equipment, and wellness apps.

- **Environmental Sustainability:** Consumers are increasingly concerned about the environment and the impact of their actions on the planet. This trend has led to a demand for eco-friendly products and services that are sustainably sourced, packaged, and manufactured.

- **Technology:** Technology is transforming the way people interact with products and services. Consumers increasingly use social media, mobile devices, and other digital platforms to research, purchase, and review products and services.

- **Economic Factors:** Economic factors such as income, employment, and inflation also impact consumer behavior. Economic changes can affect consumers' purchasing power and their willingness to spend money.

Entrepreneurs who understand these cultural and social changes can develop products and services that are more aligned with their target audience. They can also develop marketing campaigns that speak to the values and beliefs of their customers. By keeping up with the latest trends and changes in consumer behavior, entrepreneurs can stay ahead of the competition and build successful businesses.

Political Changes

Political changes refer to the transformations that occur in the political system of a country or region, which may result in new laws, policies, regulations, or changes in the government's leadership or structure. Political changes can shape entrepreneurship and the business environment in general. Political stability and the absence of corruption are crucial for entrepreneurs as they affect the ease of doing business, the level of investment, and the overall economic climate.

For instance, changes in government policies, such as tax laws, trade agreements, and subsidies, can either create opportunities or hinder the growth of businesses. Additionally, political instability and security concerns can lead to reduced investment and economic activities, which may impact consumer behavior, resulting in a shift in demand for goods and services.

Moreover, political changes can result in increased regulations, which may impact the operations of businesses, especially in highly regulated industries such as healthcare and finance. Furthermore, changes in government leadership can bring in a new set of economic ideologies that may affect the country's economy and entrepreneurial activities.

Overall, entrepreneurs must stay informed of political changes to make the necessary adjustments and take advantage of opportunities as they arise. They must also engage with policymakers and advocate for policies that support entrepreneurship and a conducive business environment. Understanding political changes is crucial for entrepreneurs to plan and make strategic decisions that will enable their businesses to thrive.

AN ANALYSIS OF CURRENT POLITICAL TRENDS IN THE U.S.

The political landscape in the U.S. is constantly changing and can influence entrepreneurship. Currently, the country is experiencing several political trends that are shaping the business environment. One major trend is the increased focus on environmental policies and regulations, particularly around climate change. The Biden administration has made climate change a top priority, leading to increased attention on sustainable and renewable energy sources and more stringent regulations around carbon emissions.

Another political trend is the push for social justice and equity. The Black Lives Matter movement and other social justice initiatives have gained significant momentum in recent years, resulting in increased scrutiny on businesses to address issues of racial and social inequality. Companies are expected to take a stance on these issues and make a concerted effort to create more diverse and inclusive workplaces.

The ongoing COVID-19 pandemic has also transformed politics and entrepreneurship. The pandemic has led to increased government intervention in the economy, particularly around issues like stimulus spending and small business relief. Additionally, the pandemic has brought to light issues around healthcare and access to affordable medical care, which may have long-term implications for the healthcare industry and related businesses.

The ongoing debate around immigration policy is another political trend that is impacting entrepreneurship. The U.S. has historically been a nation of immigrants, and many entrepreneurs have come to the country to start their businesses. However, recent changes in immigration policy have made it more difficult for entrepreneurs to obtain visas or start businesses in the U.S. This has led to increased interest in alternative locations, such as Canada, for entrepreneurs seeking to start new ventures.

Finally, the ongoing political polarization in the U.S. shapes entrepreneurship. The deep divisions in the country have led to increased scrutiny on businesses and their political affiliations, as well as concerns around the impact of political uncertainty on the economy. This has resulted in a more complex and challenging business environment for entrepreneurs.

UNDERSTANDING HOW POLITICAL CHANGES IMPACT CONSUMER BEHAVIOR

Changes in politics can sway consumer behavior in the U.S. by altering the regulatory environment, affecting the economy, and shaping people's attitudes and beliefs. Here are some examples:

- **Taxes**: Tax policies can affect consumer behavior by changing the disposable income of households. Lower taxes can result in more disposable income, leading to increased consumer spending. In contrast, higher taxes can reduce disposable income, lowering consumer spending. Taxes can also alter consumer behavior by impacting the pricing of goods and services.

- **Government Spending**: Changes in government spending can influence the economy, which in turn affects consumer behavior. For example, increased government spending on infrastructure projects can create jobs and stimulate economic growth, leading to increased consumer spending. Decreased government spending can slowdown the economy and lower consumer spending.

- **Attitudes and Beliefs**: Political changes can also shape people's attitudes and beliefs and influence their purchasing decisions. For example, changes in government policies around social issues such as climate change, human rights, and equality can influence people's perceptions of products and companies. Entrepreneurs can respond to these changes by developing products and services that align with changing values and beliefs.

- **International Trade**: Changes in government policies related to international trade can also impact consumer behavior. For example, tariffs and trade restrictions can increase the cost of imported goods, resulting in higher prices for consumers. Changes in trade policies can also create opportunities for entrepreneurs who can develop new products and services that leverage changes in global markets.

Overall, political changes can sway consumer behavior in the U.S. Entrepreneurs who can adapt to changing political and regulatory environments can seize opportunities to develop new products and services that meet evolving consumer needs.

Regulatory Changes

Regulatory changes refer to the updates or revisions made to laws and rules that impact various aspects of business operations. These changes can occur at the local, state, or federal level and may have a significant impact on entrepreneurship. The main goal of regulatory changes is to provide a framework for businesses to operate in an ethical, legal, and safe manner.

The influence of regulatory changes on entrepreneurship can be both positive and negative. On the one hand, these changes can create a more level playing field for businesses to compete in, promote innovation, and encourage new market entrants. On the other hand, regulatory changes can lead to increased costs, decreased efficiency, and stifling of innovation.

The impact of regulatory changes on entrepreneurship is highly dependent on the specific industry and type of business. For example, new regulations in the healthcare industry may make it more difficult for new entrants to start businesses due to the high level of regulatory compliance required, while regulations in the food industry may create new market opportunities for businesses that specialize in healthier options.

Overall, regulatory changes can alter the entrepreneurial landscape, and entrepreneurs need to stay up to date on those changes and their potential impact on their businesses. It is also essential for entrepreneurs to engage with regulatory bodies and policymakers to advocate for policies that promote entrepreneurship and protect the interests of businesses.

In recent years, there have been several regulatory changes that have affected entrepreneurship in the U.S. For example, changes in the tax code have changed the financial structures of businesses and incentivized certain types of investment. Additionally, changes to immigration policy have impacted the ability of businesses to hire and retain highly skilled workers. The ongoing debate around net neutrality and the regulation of technology companies is also a key area of interest for entrepreneurs as changes in this area can have substantial implications for their ability to reach customers and operate efficiently.

AN ANALYSIS OF CURRENT REGULATORY TRENDS IN THE U.S.

The United States has a complex regulatory environment that affects many industries and businesses, and regulatory trends can have a profound influence on entrepreneurship. In recent years, several regulatory changes have been implemented or proposed that could affect entrepreneurs and their ventures.

One major regulatory trend is the increasing scrutiny of big tech companies. The federal government and some state governments have launched investigations into the practices of companies like Google, Facebook, and Amazon. These investigations could lead to increased regulation of these companies, which could create opportunities for smaller players to enter the market and offer alternative services.

Another trend is the increasing focus on data privacy and security. The European Union's General Data Protection Regulation (GDPR) has spurred similar efforts in the U.S., with states like California and Virginia passing their own privacy laws. These laws can affect how businesses collect, store, and use customer data, and could lead to increased costs for compliance.

Environmental regulations are also an important trend to watch. The Biden administration has made it a priority to address climate change and has proposed several new regulations aimed at reducing greenhouse gas emissions. These regulations could create new opportunities for entrepreneurs in fields like renewable energy and energy efficiency, while also increasing costs for industries that rely heavily on fossil fuels.

Finally, labor regulations are an area of ongoing debate and change. The Department of Labor has proposed new rules on gig worker classification, which could have significant implications for companies like Uber and Lyft. Meanwhile, the federal minimum wage has not been raised in over a decade, and several states and municipalities have passed their own minimum wage laws. These changes can affect the costs of labor for businesses and can sway the business models of certain industries.

In summary, regulatory trends are an important consideration for entrepreneurs, as they can create opportunities or pose challenges for businesses. Keeping up with the latest regulatory changes and potential changes is essential for entrepreneurs who want to stay ahead of the curve and take advantage of emerging opportunities.

How the Changes in Industry Regulations Impact Entrepreneurship and Business in General

Industry regulations are rules or laws that businesses operating in a particular industry must follow. Regulatory changes refer to alterations in the rules or laws that govern the operations of businesses in a specific industry. These changes can shape entrepreneurship and business in general in the U.S.

Regulatory changes are often implemented to address concerns related to the safety, health, and well-being of the general public. For example, the introduction of new regulations in the financial industry following the 2008 global financial crisis was aimed at preventing similar crises from occurring in the future. Similarly, the introduction of new regulations in the pharmaceutical industry is aimed at ensuring that drugs are safe and effective for human use.

The influence of regulatory changes on entrepreneurship and business in general can be significant. For example, regulatory changes can create new opportunities for businesses that are well positioned to adapt to the new routines, methods, and protocols. On the other hand, they can create challenges for businesses that are inflexible and unable to alter their business plans to comply with the new regulations. For example, a business that is legally bound in a contract with a supplier of artificial chemical cleaners might run into problems if new regulations require them to use environmentally friendly, organic products instead.

In addition to creating new opportunities and challenges, regulatory changes can also have financial implications for businesses. Compliance with new regulations can be costly, as businesses may need to invest in new equipment, processes, or staff to remain in compliance. Failure to comply with new regulations can also result in fines and other financial penalties, which can be significant.

218

Entrepreneurs who are starting new businesses need to be aware of the regulatory environment in their industry. They need to stay informed about the regulatory changes that are taking place and be prepared to adapt to these changes. In addition, entrepreneurs need to be aware of the compliance requirements for their industry and take steps to ensure that they follow all relevant regulations. success of the business.

How Warby Parker Adapted to Macroeconomic Changes

The story of Warby Parker, an online eyewear company founded in 2010, is a prime example of a successful entrepreneurial venture that adapted to macroeconomic changes.

At the time of Warby Parker's entry into the eyewear industry, the market was dominated by a few major players, and prices for eyeglasses were notoriously high. Warby Parker identified the opportunity to provide affordable, high-quality eyewear through a direct-to-consumer online model. They offered a wide selection of stylish frames and partnered with a network of independent optometrists for eye exams. By offering an innovative product at a competitive price point, Warby Parker quickly gained traction and disrupted the traditional eyewear industry.

Warby Parker's success was not only due to its innovative business model but also its ability to adapt to macroeconomic changes. In 2013, the company opened its first brick-and-mortar store in New York City. This move was in response to the changing shopping behaviors of its target audience, which showed a growing preference for the in-store shopping experience. Warby Parker's physical retail locations allowed customers to try on frames in person and receive guidance from knowledgeable staff. In addition, Warby Parker's retail locations also provided the company with an opportunity to collect data on consumer preferences and feedback, which they could use to improve their product offerings and customer experience.

Warby Parker's success can also be attributed to their responsiveness to demographic and psychographic changes. The company's commitment to social responsibility, exemplified by their "Buy a Pair, Give a Pair" program, resonated with younger consumers who value socially conscious brands. Additionally, Warby Parker's partnerships with popular influencers and collaborations with notable brands such as the NFL and Marvel have helped the company stay relevant to customers across various demographics.

Overall, Warby Parker's success can be attributed to its ability to identify untapped opportunities in a highly competitive industry, offer a unique and innovative product, and adapt to changing macroeconomic trends, such as shifting shopping behaviors and demographic and psychographic changes. By staying ahead of the curve, Warby Parker has continued to grow and maintain a loyal customer base, making it one of the most successful entrepreneurial ventures in recent years.

THE IMPORTANCE OF UNDERSTANDING MACROECONOMIC CHANGE

Understanding macroeconomic change is important for entrepreneurial success because it provides insight into the various factors that can influence consumer behavior, business conditions, and the overall economic environment. Entrepreneurs who keep track of these macroeconomic factors are better positioned to identify opportunities and mitigate risks.

For example, demographic changes can influence the products and services that are in demand as well as the channels used to reach customers. By understanding the demographics of their target audience, entrepreneurs can tailor their marketing strategies to appeal to specific age groups, ethnicities, or geographic regions.

Similarly, psychographic changes can also impact consumer behavior. Understanding changing values, beliefs, and lifestyle preferences can help entrepreneurs better position their products and services to meet the evolving needs of their target audience.

Technological changes are another important factor to consider. As new technologies emerge, they can disrupt entire industries, creating opportunities for new businesses to enter the market or threatening the viability of existing ones. Entrepreneurs who keep up with technological changes can take advantage of emerging trends to gain a competitive edge.

Societal changes, such as the growing emphasis on sustainability and social responsibility, can also impact consumer behavior and the overall business environment. Entrepreneurs who take these societal trends into account can build businesses that align with these values and gain the support of socially conscious consumers.

Political changes and regulatory trends can also transform the business environment. Changes in government policies and regulations can create new opportunities or barriers for entrepreneurs. By staying informed about these changes, entrepreneurs can adjust their strategies and operations to ensure compliance and take advantage of new opportunities that arise.

In addition to the above, macroeconomic changes can also impact the availability of capital, labor, and other resources. For instance, changes in interest rates, inflation, or exchange rates can affect the cost of borrowing, the value of the currency, and other financial factors that alter business decisions. Entrepreneurs who stay abreast of these changes can make informed decisions about when to invest, when to expand, and when to hold off on business activities.

Overall, understanding macroeconomic change is critical for entrepreneurial success. By keeping track of demographic, psychographic, technological, societal, political, and regulatory trends, entrepreneurs can identify new opportunities, mitigate risks, and make informed business decisions that position them for success.

How Future Macroeconomic Changes in the U.S. Can Present Opportunities for New Startup Companies

The outlook of macroeconomic change in the United States presents several opportunities for new startup companies. One of the biggest demographic changes that will take place in the coming years is the aging of the baby boomer generation. This presents an opportunity for startups that cater to the needs and preferences of this generation, such as home healthcare services, retirement homes, and financial planning services.

In terms of psychographic changes, there is a growing trend of consumers seeking environmentally friendly and sustainable products. This presents an opportunity for startups that focus on eco-friendly products and services, such as electric cars, organic food, and sustainable fashion.

Technological changes will continue to disrupt many industries, creating new opportunities for startups. The adoption of blockchain technology, for example, presents opportunities for startups that can leverage this technology to create innovative solutions in finance, healthcare, and logistics.

Societal changes will also create opportunities for startups that can address the changing needs and preferences of consumers. For example, there is a growing demand for remote work and flexible work arrangements, which presents opportunities for startups that offer remote work solutions, such as virtual office spaces and remote team management tools.

Political changes and regulatory changes will continue to impact the business landscape in the United States. The changing political climate presents opportunities for startups that can provide solutions to challenges faced by government agencies and institutions. This could include startups that focus on cybersecurity, privacy protection, and other areas of national security.

Overall, the outlook of macroeconomic change in the United States presents a wide range of opportunities for new startup companies. Entrepreneurs who can identify and capitalize on these opportunities will be well-positioned for success in the years to come.

Summary

In summary, understanding macroeconomic change is critical for entrepreneurial success. Entrepreneurs who keep a close eye on macroeconomic factors and their impact on the market are better positioned to take advantage of opportunities and avoid costly mistakes. The following are key takeaways on the trends in the elements of macroeconomic change discussed earlier:

Demographic changes are significant drivers of change in the market. Trends such as an aging population, increased diversity, and changing family structures can impact demand for products and services, as well as the marketing strategies used to reach specific segments of the market.

Psychographic changes are important to entrepreneurs because they can impact customer preferences, buying behaviors, and brand loyalty. Entrepreneurs who take into account the values, beliefs, and lifestyles of their target customers are better able to create products and services that resonate with their needs and wants.

Technological changes are a double-edged sword, presenting both opportunities and challenges. Entrepreneurs who stay ahead of emerging technologies are better positioned to disrupt the market and take advantage of new opportunities. At the same time, technologies can also disrupt established businesses, making it imperative for entrepreneurs to keep up with industry trends and stay innovative.

Societal changes are another factor that entrepreneurs must understand to stay competitive. Changes in social norms, attitudes, and beliefs can impact the market for products and services, as well as the marketing strategies used to reach consumers.

Political changes can also impact the market in significant ways, particularly when it comes to government policies and regulations. Entrepreneurs who stay up to date with the latest policy developments can position their businesses to take advantage of new opportunities and avoid costly regulatory risks.

Finally, regulatory changes can have a significant impact on entrepreneurial success. Changes in laws and regulations can create new market opportunities, but they can also impose new compliance costs and create new risks for businesses. Entrepreneurs who stay ahead of regulatory developments are better positioned to navigate these challenges and take advantage of new opportunities.

In summary, understanding macroeconomic change is critical for entrepreneurial success. Entrepreneurs who stay informed and take a proactive approach to these trends can gain a competitive advantage in the market and build successful businesses.

13. Competition

You have to have an international reference of competition.

You have to have the highest [standards].

Carlos Slim

Founder of Grupo Carso

Assessing industry condition and industry status provides a starting point for understanding competition. To outperform the competition, the *learning curve, complementary assets,* and *reputation effects* are key factors for entrepreneurs to understand. This is the competition element of the Opportunity Analysis Canvas.

The Opportunity Analysis Canvas

Emphasis on "Competition"

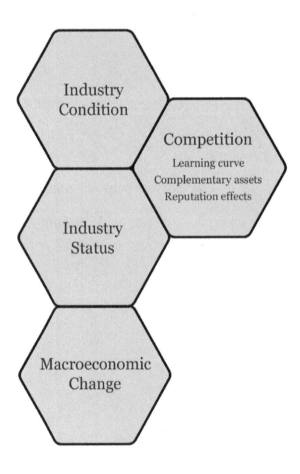

Competition is a key factor in entrepreneurship. As an entrepreneur, understanding competition is essential to make informed business decisions and to sustain a successful business. Competition provides an opportunity to identify a business niche, understand market trends, and anticipate customer preferences. By understanding the competitive landscape, entrepreneurs can develop strategies that can help them stay ahead of the competition.

One of the key reasons why understanding competition is important is that it can help entrepreneurs identify gaps in the market that they can exploit. By understanding the offerings of competitors, entrepreneurs can identify areas where there is a need for new and innovative products or services. This can help entrepreneurs to identify their unique selling proposition (USP), which can set them apart from their competitors.

Understanding competition can also help entrepreneurs anticipate customer preferences. Through studying competitor offerings and analyzing customer behavior, entrepreneurs can develop products or services that better serve customer needs. This can help them remain competitive and maintain a loyal customer base.

Additionally, understanding competition can help entrepreneurs make informed business decisions. By analyzing competitor strategies, entrepreneurs can identify their strengths and weaknesses and develop strategies to take advantage of these. This can help entrepreneurs to make decisions that are in line with market trends and consumer preferences, which can ultimately lead to business success.

Overall, understanding competition is critical for entrepreneurs. By staying informed of industry trends and analyzing competitors, entrepreneurs can develop unique strategies, identify gaps in the market, and anticipate customer preferences. This can help them make informed business decisions that are in line with market trends, and ultimately lead to business success.

The Learning Curve

The learning curve is a concept that describes the relationship between the amount of experience or practice someone has with a task and their ability to perform that task efficiently and effectively. As individuals or companies gain experience in performing a task, they become more efficient and productive, which can reduce production costs and increase the final product's quality. For entrepreneurs, understanding the learning curve is crucial to ensuring they remain competitive.

Entrepreneurs can apply the learning concept to various aspects of their businesses. For example, an entrepreneur may consider the learning curve when hiring employees or training existing staff. Hiring employees with prior experience can reduce the time it takes to train them, enabling them to become productive more quickly, whereas hiring unskilled workers will result in a longer learning curve, meaning a slower start to productivity and increased training costs. Furthermore, entrepreneurs may apply the concept of the learning curve to product development. By making incremental improvements to their product, entrepreneurs can reduce the time it takes to produce it and lower production costs.

The learning curve concept can also help entrepreneurs to identify opportunities to improve their products and processes. By analyzing the performance of a product or process over time, entrepreneurs can identify trends that may suggest that the learning curve is still active or has plateaued. Entrepreneurs can then take appropriate measures to improve the product or process and reduce the time and cost of production. For example, entrepreneurs may invest in new technology or better training for employees to help accelerate the learning curve.

In conclusion, the learning curve is a crucial concept for entrepreneurs as it allows them to understand the relationship between experience, productivity, and cost of production. Understanding the learning curve can help entrepreneurs identify opportunities to improve their products and processes, hire employees more efficiently, and reduce the time and cost of production. By optimizing the learning curve, entrepreneurs can achieve a competitive advantage in their industry.

HOW THE LEARNING CURVE IMPACTS COMPETITION

The learning curve is an important concept for entrepreneurs to understand when analyzing competition. It refers to the idea that as a company produces more of a product, it becomes more efficient at doing so. This increased efficiency leads to a reduction in the unit cost of production. In other words, the more a company produces, the cheaper it becomes to produce each unit. This cost reduction creates a competitive advantage for companies that can take advantage of it.

The learning curve is particularly important in industries with high fixed costs and low variable costs. This is because the cost savings from the learning curve are mostly associated with the variable costs. In contrast, fixed costs, such as capital equipment or buildings, are generally constant and not affected by changes in production volume. Industries that fit this description include manufacturing, transportation, and software development.

Companies that can take advantage of the learning curve have a significant competitive advantage over those that cannot. This is because they can offer their products at lower prices, which makes them more attractive to consumers. Lower prices can also help companies gain market share and increase their profits. Companies that are unable to take advantage of the learning curve are at a disadvantage because their costs remain high, making their products less competitive in the marketplace.

One way for companies to take advantage of the learning curve is to focus on scale. By increasing production volume, a company can benefit from the cost savings associated with the learning curve. However, achieving scale requires significant investment in infrastructure and production capabilities. This can be a challenge for startups and small businesses.

Another way for companies to take advantage of the learning curve is to focus on efficiency. Companies can increase production efficiency and reduce costs by continuously improving processes and reducing waste.

In summary, the learning curve is an important concept for entrepreneurs to understand because it provides a pathway to achieving a competitive advantage through cost reduction. Companies that take advantage of the learning curve can offer their products at lower prices, which makes them more attractive to consumers and helps them gain market share.

Successful Startup Companies That Utilized the Learning Curve Effectively to Enter a New Market

Many successful startup companies have effectively utilized the learning curve to enter new markets. Here are a few:

- **Amazon**: When Amazon first entered the book market, it had to learn about the industry, the supply chain, and customer behavior. By the time it started expanding into other product categories, it had already developed expertise in logistics, customer data analysis, and online retail. This allowed it to scale up quickly and become a dominant force in e-commerce.
- **Airbnb**: When Airbnb first started, it was a small platform for renting out air mattresses in people's homes. Over time, the company learned how to build trust between hosts and guests, price listings, and provide a consistent user experience. This allowed it to expand into new markets and compete with traditional hotels.
- **Tesla**: When Tesla first started making electric cars, it had to learn about battery technology, charging infrastructure, and manufacturing processes. By the time it released its Model S sedan, the company had developed a deep understanding of the market and was able to deliver a high-quality product that outperformed its competitors.

In each of these examples, the learning curve played a crucial role in the success of the startup company. By taking the time to understand the market, supply chain, and customer behavior, these companies were able to develop a competitive advantage that allowed them to scale up quickly and outperform their rivals.

STRATEGIES THAT ENTREPRENEURS CAN USE TO TAKE ADVANTAGE OF THE LEARNING CURVE

Entrepreneurs can use several strategies to take advantage of the learning curve and increase their competitive advantage. Here are a few examples:

- **Focus on Specialization**: Entrepreneurs should consider specializing in a particular product or service to gain a deeper understanding of that area. By focusing on a niche market, entrepreneurs can develop expertise and learn more quickly, leading to a faster and more efficient learning curve. Specialization also helps to differentiate a product or service from competitors and attract a specific customer base.

- **Collaborate with Industry Experts**: Working with experts in a particular field can accelerate the learning curve. By collaborating with industry leaders, entrepreneurs can learn from their expertise and experience. This can include working with mentors, industry associations, and networking with other entrepreneurs in the field.

- **Implement a Continuous Learning Culture**: Entrepreneurs can encourage a culture of continuous learning in their organizations to promote skill development and knowledge sharing. By offering training and professional development opportunities, entrepreneurs can help their team members develop new skills and stay up to date with industry trends.

- **Embrace Failure**: Failure is an essential component of the learning curve. Entrepreneurs willing to take risks and learn from their mistakes will ultimately be more successful than those who are risk averse. Entrepreneurs should be open to trying new ideas, even if they are uncertain about the outcome.

- **Leverage Technology**: Technology can help entrepreneurs streamline and automate various processes, accelerating the learning curve. For example, data analytics can help entrepreneurs gain insights into customer behavior and market trends, allowing them to adjust their strategies accordingly.

In conclusion, understanding the learning curve and implementing strategies to take advantage of it is essential for entrepreneurs. By focusing on specialization, collaborating with industry experts, implementing a culture of continuous learning, embracing failure, and leveraging technology, entrepreneurs can gain a competitive advantage and achieve long-term success.

Complementary Assets

Complementary assets refer to assets or resources that are required to extract the full value from a product or service. These assets can include anything from equipment, software, or services to relationships with suppliers or customers and the knowledge and expertise of a workforce. In other words, complementary assets are the supporting resources that are needed to create, market, distribute, and service a product or service and to create value for the customer.

Complementary assets are important for entrepreneurs because they can help to create a competitive advantage. By acquiring or developing the right complementary assets, entrepreneurs can differentiate their product or service from competitors and create more value for customers. For example, a company that develops a new software application may need to partner with hardware manufacturers or internet service providers to ensure that the application runs smoothly and is accessible to users. The partnership with complementary asset providers can create a more robust and valuable product for customers.

Complementary assets are also important because they can impact the cost of production and distribution. For example, a company that owns its own manufacturing facilities or has exclusive relationships with suppliers may be able to produce goods at a lower cost than competitors who do not have those complementary assets. This can allow the company to offer a more competitive price to customers, or to reinvest those cost savings in other areas of the business, such as research and development or marketing.

In addition, complementary assets can create barriers to entry for competitors. By acquiring or developing key complementary assets, entrepreneurs can make it more difficult for competitors to enter the market or to create a similar product or service. For example, a company that has exclusive relationships with key suppliers may be able to prevent competitors from accessing those suppliers or may be able to negotiate more favorable terms with those suppliers than competitors can. This can make it more difficult for competitors to match the product or service offering, creating a competitive advantage for the company with the complementary assets.

How Complementary Assets Impact Competition

Complementary assets are critical for entrepreneurs seeking to establish themselves in competitive markets. Complementary assets refer to resources, capabilities, and products that are necessary to enhance the value of an entrepreneur's product or service. These assets can range from technology to manufacturing capabilities, customer data, marketing, distribution, and even intellectual property. Using complementary assets can differentiate an entrepreneur from their competitors by providing a unique value proposition, increasing market share, and improving profitability.

Complementary assets are crucial in determining a company's position in the market and can provide competitive advantages to the entrepreneurs who have them. For example, in the mobile phone industry, Apple's complementary assets, including its software and hardware integration, extensive app store, strong branding, and retail stores, have been key to its success. Other players in the mobile phone industry have found it challenging to replicate these complementary assets.

Another example is Amazon's complementary assets, including its logistics and distribution capabilities, vast customer database, and large market share. These assets have enabled Amazon to expand into new markets such as cloud computing, online streaming, and smart home devices, where the company has leveraged its existing complementary assets.

Complementary assets also impact competition by affecting the cost structure of a business. For example, if an entrepreneur can leverage an existing infrastructure to deliver their product or service, it can significantly lower production and distribution costs. This r can lead to higher profit margins, which can be used to fund further expansion, research, and development.

In summary, complementary assets play a vital role in the competition as entrepreneurs seek to differentiate themselves from their competitors. They can provide unique value propositions, enhance market share, and impact the cost structure of a business. Entrepreneurs should focus on identifying and acquiring the necessary complementary assets to build a sustainable competitive advantage.

SUCCESSFUL STARTUP COMPANIES THAT UTILIZED COMPLEMENTARY ASSETS EFFECTIVELY TO ENTER A NEW MARKET

Complementary assets are key resources or capabilities that are needed to enable a firm's primary resources or capabilities to create value. For example, a firm may have innovative technology but lack the sales and marketing capabilities to effectively bring its products to market. In such cases, the firm needs to acquire the complementary assets that are needed to exploit its core strengths. Here are a few examples of successful startup companies that utilized complementary assets effectively:

- **Instagram**: Instagram was able to gain a large user base quickly by leveraging the complementary assets of its parent company, Facebook. Instagram's core strength was its photo-sharing app, which was highly valued by users. However, the company lacked the resources to build a large user base on its own. By leveraging Facebook's existing user base and advertising platform, Instagram quickly grew its user base and became one of the most popular social media platforms ever.

- **Tesla**: Tesla's core strength is its innovative electric vehicle technology. However, the company needed to acquire complementary assets, such as battery manufacturing and charging infrastructure, to make its electric cars more practical and attractive to customers. Tesla invested heavily in building its own battery manufacturing plant and charging network, allowing it to offer customers a complete electric vehicle ecosystem.

- **Uber**: Uber is a classic example of a company that leveraged complementary assets to enter a new market. Uber's core strength was its innovative ride-hailing app, which disrupted the traditional taxi industry. However, the company needed to acquire complementary assets, such as drivers, vehicles, and insurance, to be able to provide a high-quality service. Uber was able to attract a large number of drivers by offering them the opportunity to earn money flexibly, and the company provided insurance coverage to ensure passenger safety.

In each of these cases, the successful startup company was able to leverage complementary assets to overcome the challenges of entering a new market and create value for customers.

STRATEGIES THAT ENTREPRENEURS CAN USE TO ACQUIRE COMPLEMENTARY ASSETS

Complementary assets are an important factor that entrepreneurs must consider when entering a new market. Complementary assets refer to any resource or asset that a company needs to succeed in the market but cannot generate on its own. For example, complementary assets for a software company might include a well-known brand name, a large customer base, or patents. Complementary assets can also include strategic partnerships with other companies or access to distribution channels. Entrepreneurs must acquire complementary assets to compete effectively in the market.

One strategy for acquiring complementary assets is establishing strategic partnerships with other companies. For example, a startup that creates a new technology might partner with an established company to gain access to its distribution channels. The established company might also provide marketing support and help with brand recognition. In return, the startup might offer the established company an equity stake or some other benefit.

Another strategy for acquiring complementary assets is to acquire other companies. For example, a startup might acquire a company with an established brand name or a large customer base. This can help the startup gain a foothold in the market and increase its chances of success.

Entrepreneurs can also license or purchase patents to gain access to complementary assets. Patents can provide legal protection for a company's intellectual property and prevent competitors from using similar technology. By licensing or purchasing patents, entrepreneurs can acquire the necessary intellectual property to compete effectively in the market.

Finally, entrepreneurs can build their own complementary assets by investing in marketing and brand recognition. For example, a startup might create a viral marketing campaign to increase brand recognition and attract customers. This can help the startup establish itself in the market and compete effectively with established companies.

In summary, acquiring complementary assets is an important strategy for entrepreneurs to compete effectively in the market. Entrepreneurs can establish strategic partnerships with other companies, acquire other companies, license, or purchase patents, or build their own complementary assets through marketing and brand recognition.

Reputation Effects

Reputation effects refer to the positive or negative perceptions that customers and stakeholders have of a business based on its past behavior and performance. Reputation can be an important factor in influencing consumer behavior and affecting a company's level of competition it faces. In the context of entrepreneurship, a positive reputation can be particularly important for new and emerging companies, as they may not have a well-established track record or brand recognition.

Reputation effects can impact competition in several ways. A strong reputation can help a company to differentiate itself from competitors and establish a competitive advantage. It can also help to build customer loyalty and increase customer retention rates, which can, in turn, lead to increased sales and revenue. On the other hand, a negative reputation can be detrimental to a company's competitiveness, leading to reduced sales, difficulty in attracting investment or partnership, and difficulty in attracting and retaining talented employees.

Reputation effects are particularly important in industries where trust and credibility are key factors in consumer decision making. For example, in the financial services industry, a company's reputation for honesty, reliability, and good customer service can be critical in attracting and retaining customers. In the healthcare industry, reputation can be a key factor in building trust with patients and healthcare providers, impacting a company's ability to partner with other healthcare organizations.

Several successful startup companies have leveraged reputation effects to build their businesses. For example, online retailer Amazon has built a reputation for fast, reliable shipping, excellent customer service, and competitive pricing, which has helped it to become one of the most successful e-commerce companies in the world. Similarly, Tesla built a strong reputation for innovation, sustainability, and performance in the electric vehicle market, which has helped it to attract a loyal customer base and establish itself as a leading player in the industry.

Entrepreneurs can leverage reputation effects by building strong relationships with customers and stakeholders, delivering high-quality products and services, and being transparent and accountable in their business practices. They can also build their reputation by partnering with well-respected companies or organizations and by engaging in activities that demonstrate their commitment to social responsibility and ethical business practices. By focusing on building a strong reputation, entrepreneurs can differentiate themselves from competitors, build customer loyalty, and establish a competitive advantage in their industry.

HOW REPUTATION IMPACTS COMPETITION

Reputation can significantly impact competition in any industry. A positive reputation can help a company attract customers and partners, while a negative reputation can lead to distrust and lost business. A company's reputation is based on its performance, ethics, brand identity, customer satisfaction, and other factors. Reputation can be built and maintained over time and is often viewed as an asset for a company.

Reputation impacts competition in several ways. First, a company with a good reputation is more likely to attract customers, as customers tend to trust and prefer companies with a positive track record. A good reputation can also help a company build relationships with suppliers and partners, which can help the company access new markets and resources.

Second, a company with a good reputation is more likely to be able to charge premium prices for its products or services. Customers are often willing to pay more for products and services that they perceive as being of higher quality, and a company with a good reputation is often seen as providing such products or services.

Third, a company with a good reputation can weather negative events more easily. For example, if a company experiences a product recall or other negative event, customers and partners may be more forgiving if the company has a strong reputation for quality and ethical behavior.

On the other hand, a company with a negative reputation may struggle to attract customers and partners, possibly being forced to compete on price rather than quality. A negative reputation can also lead to regulatory and legal challenges and result in fines, settlements, and other financial losses.

In conclusion, reputation is a critical factor that impacts competition, as it can determine a company's ability to attract customers, charge premium prices, and build relationships with partners and suppliers. Entrepreneurs need to be aware of the importance of reputation and work to build and maintain a positive image to succeed in the competitive market.

Successful Startup Companies That Utilized Reputation Effects Effectively

Reputation effects can play a critical role in the success of a startup company. When a company establishes a strong reputation, it can differentiate itself from competitors and build customer loyalty, leading to sustained growth over time. Here are a few examples of companies that have effectively leveraged reputation effects:

- **Glossier**: Glossier, a beauty and skincare brand, capitalized on the power of reputation effects by leveraging social media and user-generated content. The company prioritized building a community of engaged customers and brand advocates through its inclusive and transparent approach to beauty. Glossier encouraged customers to share their experiences and opinions through social media, resulting in a flood of positive reviews, testimonials, and user-generated content. This organic, word-of-mouth marketing fueled Glossier's growth and cemented its reputation as a brand that listens to its customers, resulting in a dedicated and loyal customer base.
- **Impossible Foods**: Impossible Foods, a company specializing in plant-based meat alternatives, successfully utilized reputation effects to disrupt the traditional meat industry. By focusing on

creating meat-like products that mimic the taste and texture of animal-based meat, Impossible Foods garnered attention and built a reputation for innovation and sustainability. The company's flagship product, the Impossible Burger, gained positive reviews from both vegans and meat-eaters, attracting widespread media coverage and consumer interest. Impossible Foods' reputation as a company committed to creating sustainable and delicious alternatives to traditional meat helped it secure partnerships with major restaurant chains and expand its market presence rapidly.

- **Patagonia**: Patagonia has built a reputation as a socially responsible and environmentally sustainable company with a strong commitment to ethical manufacturing and conservation. This reputation has helped the company attract a dedicated customer base that values these same principles. As a result, Patagonia has grown its business while remaining true to its core values.

Building a strong reputation can be a powerful way for a startup company to differentiate itself from competitors and build customer loyalty. This can be especially important in crowded or competitive markets where it can be difficult to stand out based on price or features alone.

STRATEGIES THAT ENTREPRENEURS CAN USE TO BUILD A STRONG REPUTATION

A strong reputation can be a key differentiator for an entrepreneur in a competitive market. Here are some strategies entrepreneurs can use to build a strong reputation:

- **Provide Exceptional Customer Service**: Providing excellent customer service is an essential component of building a strong reputation. When customers have a positive experience with a business, they are more likely to recommend it to others and leave positive reviews.

- **Focus On Quality**: Providing high-quality products or services can help establish a business as a leader in its industry. Customers are more likely to trust a company that consistently produces quality products or services.

- **Build a Strong Brand**: A strong brand can help a business stand out in a crowded market. Entrepreneurs should focus on developing a brand that communicates the unique value proposition of their business and resonates with their target market.

- **Network and Build Relationships**: Building relationships with other entrepreneurs, industry experts, and customers can help an entrepreneur establish a positive reputation. Entrepreneurs can attend industry events, participate in online forums, and seek out opportunities to connect with others in their industry.

- **Be Transparent and Honest**: Transparency and honesty are critical to building a strong reputation. Entrepreneurs should be transparent about their business practices and honest with their customers.

- **Leverage Social Media**: Social media can be a powerful tool for building a strong reputation. Entrepreneurs can use social media platforms to engage with customers, share their stories, and build their brands.

- **Give Back to the Community**: Giving back to the community can help an entrepreneur establish a positive reputation. Entrepreneurs can donate a portion of their profits to a charitable organization, sponsor community events, or volunteer their time to support local initiatives.

Building a strong reputation takes time and effort. Entrepreneurs should focus on providing exceptional customer service, producing high-quality products or services, building a strong brand, networking, being transparent and honest, leveraging social media, and giving back to the community to establish a positive reputation and gain a competitive advantage.

How the Learning Curve, Complementary Assets, and Reputation Effects of Competition Work Together

The learning curve, complementary assets, and reputation effects are key factors for entrepreneurs to consider when entering a new market and competing with established players. These elements are interrelated and can work together to create a competitive advantage for entrepreneurs.

The learning curve can lead to improvements in the efficiency of operations, which can be complemented by acquiring complementary assets. This can lead to the development of a strong reputation because the entrepreneur is able to provide high-quality goods or services at a lower cost than their competitors. A strong reputation, in turn, can lead to further improvements in the learning curve, as customers are more likely to return to a business that they trust.

For example, a startup in the technology industry may have a steep learning curve as they work to develop a new software product. However, if they can acquire complementary assets, such as partnerships with other technology companies or access to specialized equipment, they can improve their efficiency and time to market. As they release their product and develop a strong reputation for quality and innovation, they may find that their learning curve continues to improve, as they gain more experience and insight from customer feedback.

Another example is a startup in the retail industry that is focused on sustainability. By leveraging the learning curve to optimize their supply chain and operations, and by acquiring complementary assets such as partnerships with eco-friendly suppliers and producers, they can differentiate themselves from their competitors and build a reputation as a socially responsible business. As their reputation grows, they may find that they can negotiate better terms with suppliers and attract more customers, which can lead to further improvements in their learning curve.

In summary, the learning curve, complementary assets, and reputation effects are interrelated and can work together to create a competitive advantage for entrepreneurs. By understanding these elements and how they can be leveraged to create value for customers, entrepreneurs can position themselves for success in a competitive marketplace.

The Importance of Managing Competition for Entrepreneurial Success

Managing competition is critical for the success of entrepreneurs. In highly competitive markets, businesses must continually adapt, innovate, and differentiate their products and services to stand out. Competition heavily influences various aspects of a business, such as pricing, marketing, and sales strategy. Therefore, understanding and managing competition is a crucial aspect of any entrepreneurial endeavor.

One of the key reasons for managing competition is to maintain and increase market share. This can be achieved by focusing on building a unique value proposition that differentiates a business from its competitors. By creating a distinctive brand image and offering superior products and services, entrepreneurs can attract and retain customers. Successful entrepreneurs also leverage their brands and reputations to create loyal customer bases and gain a competitive edge.

Another important reason to manage competition is to stay abreast of market trends and emerging technologies. Entrepreneurs who keep a close eye on their competition can identify new opportunities and make necessary adjustments to their business strategies. For instance, they may learn from their competitors' mistakes and gain valuable insights into new markets, customer segments, and products. By keeping a watchful eye on the competition, entrepreneurs can make informed decisions about how to position their business for growth.

Finally, managing competition is crucial for long-term success. By continuously monitoring and adapting to changes in the competitive landscape, entrepreneurs can stay ahead of the curve and outperform their rivals. They can build strong partnerships and networks that provide them access to complementary assets and expertise, create a brand reputation that instills trust and loyalty, and implement cost-effective marketing strategies to acquire and retain customers.

In conclusion, managing competition is a critical component of entrepreneurial success. Entrepreneurs who stay abreast of market trends, understand the competitive landscape, build strong brand reputations, and value propositions have the greatest chance of long-term success. By leveraging the learning curve, complementary assets, and reputation effects, entrepreneurs can create sustainable businesses that thrive in highly competitive markets.

RECAP OF THE IMPORTANCE OF THE LEARNING CURVE, COMPLEMENTARY ASSETS, AND REPUTATION EFFECTS IN COMPETITION

The three key elements of competition in entrepreneurship are the learning curve, complementary assets, and reputation effects. The learning curve represents the cost savings from experience and skill gained over time, while complementary assets refer to resources that support and enhance the entrepreneur's core competencies. Reputation effects, on the other hand, are the advantages of having a positive brand or reputation in the market.

Entrepreneurs must understand these three elements of competition to outperform their rivals in the market. Startups that can reduce the learning curve by improving their skills and experience gain a competitive advantage by lowering costs and improving efficiency. The ability to acquire complementary assets such as resources, skills, or relationships can help the entrepreneur create value and a competitive advantage in the market. A strong reputation provides a competitive advantage by creating a sense of trust, credibility, and brand loyalty among consumers.

Several successful startups have leveraged these elements to gain a competitive advantage. For instance, Tesla's reputation for innovative technology has helped it gain a loyal customer base while also helping the company attract talent and investment. Airbnb's early focus on complementary assets such as user reviews, verified photography, and customer service helped it build a competitive advantage over traditional hotels.

Entrepreneurs can implement several strategies to take advantage of these competition elements. To manage the learning curve, they must focus on continuous improvement, knowledge sharing, and employee training. Entrepreneurs can build partnerships, strategic alliances, and collaborations with other companies to acquire complementary assets. Finally, entrepreneurs must maintain a good reputation by providing high-quality products or services, engaging with customers, and using social media to improve their brand image.

In conclusion, entrepreneurs must manage competition effectively by understanding the learning curve, complementary assets, and reputation effects. These elements work together to help entrepreneurs create value, reduce costs, build a loyal customer base, and maintain a good reputation. By implementing appropriate strategies and using these elements to their advantage, entrepreneurs can build a competitive advantage and succeed in the market.

Summary

Competition is an essential part of entrepreneurship. Through competition, entrepreneurs are driven to innovate, improve their products and services, and offer better value to their customers. By understanding the role of the learning curve, complementary assets, and reputation effects, entrepreneurs can gain a competitive advantage and succeed in their respective markets. Successful entrepreneurs not only focus on their own strengths but also analyze the competition and the market to identify opportunities for growth and improvement.

Additionally, entrepreneurs must understand the importance of managing competition to remain competitive and sustainable in the long run. By staying on top of the latest trends and advancements in their industry, entrepreneurs can position themselves as leaders and innovators in their field. Overall, competition can be a powerful driving force for entrepreneurship and is key to creating a thriving and dynamic economy.

14. Acting Entrepreneurially

An idea that is developed and put into action
is more important than an idea that exists only as an idea.

Edward de Bono

Physician, Author, and Inventor

253

With an understanding of *entrepreneurial mindset*, *entrepreneurial motivation*, and *entrepreneurial behavior*, and insights into the key industry and market forces, you are well prepared to develop your entrepreneurial ideas. Our final chapters on *value innovation* and *opportunity identification* conclude our discussion of the Opportunity Analysis Canvas.

The Opportunity Analysis Canvas

Emphasis on "Part III – Acting Entrepreneurially"

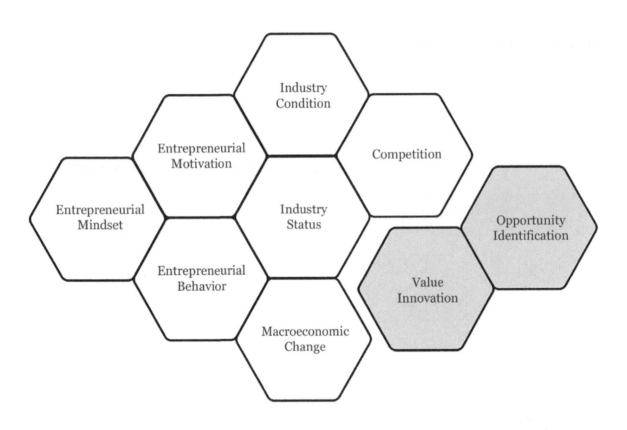

As an entrepreneur, the goal is to create value through innovation and identifying opportunities. The journey begins with an understanding of the entrepreneurial mindset, motivation, behavior, and the key industry and market forces. This chapter focuses on acting entrepreneurially by assessing two critical areas: value innovation and opportunity identification.

Value Innovation

Value innovation is the process of creating new value for customers while reducing costs. This process is different from traditional innovation, which tends to focus on improving existing products or services. As an entrepreneur, the goal is to create a new market space by identifying unmet needs and developing solutions that deliver value to customers. This is often done by introducing new products or services that are fundamentally different from what currently exists in the market.

The first step in value innovation is to identify the factors that are important to customers. This involves conducting market research and understanding customer needs and preferences. Once you understand what your customers want, the next step is to identify areas where you can create new value. This might involve developing new features, improving existing ones, or rethinking the entire product or service.

To create value innovation, entrepreneurs need to be creative and take calculated risks. This involves challenging assumptions, breaking free from established norms, and rethinking the way things have always been done. Entrepreneurs must be willing to think outside the box and explore new possibilities, even if they seem far-fetched at first. Value innovation requires a deep understanding of the market, the customer, and the competition, as well as a willingness to experiment and iterate based on feedback.

255

Opportunity Identification

Opportunity identification is the process of recognizing and developing new business ideas. Entrepreneurs need to be able to identify opportunities that have the potential for success, and then develop and execute a plan to turn those opportunities into profitable ventures.

There are several methods that entrepreneurs can use to identify opportunities. One approach is to look for problems or inefficiencies in the market that have not been addressed by existing solutions. This might involve identifying customer pain points, market gaps, or areas where existing products or services are inadequate. Another approach is to monitor emerging trends and technologies and identify opportunities to leverage these developments to create new value for customers.

Once an opportunity has been identified, the next step is to evaluate its potential for success. This involves conducting market research, assessing the competition, and evaluating the business idea's feasibility. Entrepreneurs must consider factors such as market size, profitability, scalability, and potential risks and challenges.

To turn an opportunity into a successful venture, entrepreneurs need to be able to execute on their ideas. This involves developing a solid business plan, securing funding, building a team, and executing on the plan. Successful entrepreneurs can balance risk and reward and make decisions based on data and feedback from the market.

Summary

Value innovation and opportunity identification are critical components of the entrepreneurial process. By creating new value for customers and identifying new business opportunities, entrepreneurs can develop profitable ventures and positively impact the world. Entrepreneurs need to be creative, innovative, and willing to take calculated risks to succeed. They must also be able to execute their ideas, build strong teams, and adapt to changes in the market. By understanding the importance of value innovation and opportunity identification, entrepreneurs can position themselves for success and make a difference in the world.

15. Value Innovation

We didn't reinvent the circus.

We repackaged it in a much more modern way.

Guy Laliberté

Founder of Cirque du Soliel

With big ideas and scarce resources, entrepreneurs must be efficient in their decisions and discerning in their management of time and money. The concept of *value innovation* is well suited to evaluating how to compete efficiently and effectively.

The Opportunity Analysis Canvas

Emphasis on "Value Innovation"

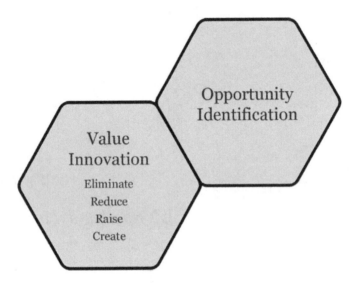

Value innovation is the parallel pursuit of product differentiation and low cost, creating a rise in value for both buyers and the company (your startup). The value to buyers is derived from the product's benefits minus its price. The value realized by the company is generated from the product's price (company revenues) minus your cost (company expenses). Value innovation is achieved when the benefits, price, and cost system is aligned.

Value innovation and value curves are linked, as discussed in the article Charting Your Company's Future. Value curves are the tool for developing and delivering value innovation. The value curve is a diagram that compares certain product or service factors on a relative scale of low to high. Factors often include features, benefits, price, brand, location, and a variety of other factors seen by customers. Diagramming each competitor's value curve alongside one another can identify value gaps and highlight opportunities for entrepreneurs.

To deliver value innovation, focus on four questions that align with what to eliminate, reduce, raise, and create within the venture. Are there select factors we can eliminate that are of limited to no real value to our target customers? A second element we'll explore is reducing factors. Are there factors on the value curve that we can reduce without significantly reducing the value delivered to customers? Another element that we'll examine is raising certain factors. Lastly, are there new factors we can create? When we look at these three questions collectively, we'll gain insights into how we can deliver value innovation to successfully compete in the marketplace.

THE IMPORTANCE OF VALUE INNOVATION FOR ENTREPRENEURS

Value innovation is critical for entrepreneurs because it is one of the key ways they can differentiate themselves from competitors and succeed in the market. When entrepreneurs achieve value innovation, they create a product or service that is unique, desirable to consumers, and cost-effective for the company. By pursuing both differentiation and cost reduction, entrepreneurs create a new value curve that sets them apart from competitors.

In today's highly competitive business landscape, it is crucial for entrepreneurs to create unique value propositions that address unmet consumer needs. This is where value innovation comes in - by creating a new value curve, entrepreneurs can offer a product or service that is truly different from what competitors are offering. This can help attract customers and build brand loyalty, which is especially important for startups trying to establish themselves in a market.

Value innovation is also important for entrepreneurs because it allows them to be cost-effective while offering a high-quality product or service. By reducing costs without sacrificing value to customers, entrepreneurs can improve their profit margins and stay competitive in the market. This is especially important for startups that may have limited resources because they need to be efficient with their spending to ensure their long-term success.

In addition, value innovation can help entrepreneurs identify new opportunities and markets. By examining the value curves of competitors, entrepreneurs can identify gaps in the market where they can offer a unique value proposition. They can also identify areas where they can improve existing products or services, creating a new value curve and differentiating themselves from competitors.

Overall, value innovation is essential for entrepreneurs to succeed in today's market. By pursuing differentiation and cost reduction simultaneously, entrepreneurs can create a new value curve that sets them apart from competitors, attracts customers, and improves their bottom line. It also allows them to identify new opportunities and stay ahead of changes in the market. By prioritizing value innovation, entrepreneurs can build a strong foundation for their startup and set themselves up for long-term success.

THE VALUE CURVE AS A TOOL FOR DEVELOPING AND DELIVERING VALUE INNOVATION

The value curve is a powerful tool that entrepreneurs can use to develop and deliver value innovation. It provides a visual representation of the features and benefits of a product or service in comparison to those of competitors. By examining these value curves, entrepreneurs can identify opportunities to create value and stand out from the competition.

The value curve is made up of a series of factors that are important to customers, such as price, quality, convenience, and customer service. These factors are plotted on a graph, with the importance of each factor represented on the Y-axis and the level of performance on the X-axis. This creates a curve that represents the value a company delivers to its customers compared to its competitors.

The Value Curve for Cirque du Soleil

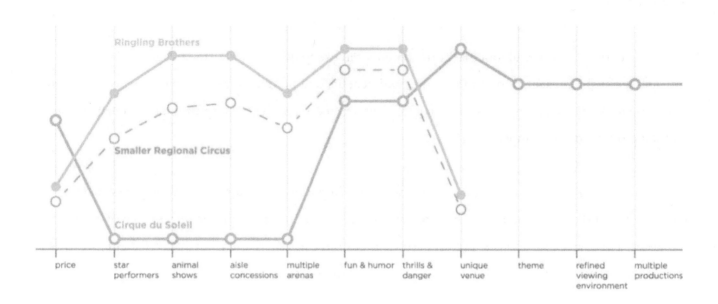

Entrepreneurs can use the value curve to identify areas where they can differentiate themselves from their competitors. For example, they may identify a factor that is highly valued by customers but poorly delivered by competitors. By focusing on this factor and improving their performance, entrepreneurs can create a new value curve that puts them ahead of competitors.

Entrepreneurs can also use the value curve to identify areas where they can reduce costs without sacrificing value. For example, they may identify a factor that is less important to customers than other factors but is still delivered at a high level by competitors. By reducing their performance in this area, entrepreneurs can save money without reducing the overall value they deliver to customers.

In addition to identifying opportunities to differentiate and reduce costs, the value curve can also be used to identify areas where entrepreneurs can create new value. By adding new features or benefits to their product or service, entrepreneurs can create a new value curve that exceeds the performance of their competitors in important areas.

The value curve is an essential tool for entrepreneurs looking to develop and deliver value innovation. By using the value curve to identify areas for differentiation, cost reduction, and value creation, entrepreneurs can create a unique value proposition that sets them apart from the competition and delivers maximum value to their customers.

1. What to Eliminate

By eliminating these factors, entrepreneurs can streamline their operations, reduce costs, and focus on delivering what customers truly value. This can create a more competitive and efficient business model that is better positioned to succeed in the marketplace.

To identify what to eliminate, entrepreneurs can thoroughly analyze the industry and the target customers. They can also gather customer feedback and use market research to understand the factors that are most important to them. By understanding what customers truly value, entrepreneurs can identify areas where they can eliminate features or services of limited value.

An example of eliminating factors can be seen in the case of Southwest Airlines, which eliminated certain amenities such as in-flight meals, assigned seating, and baggage transfers to reduce costs and focus on delivering what customers truly value - low fares, on-time arrivals, and hassle-free travel. This strategy has helped Southwest become one of the most successful and profitable airlines in the industry.

In summary, "what to eliminate" is a key element of value innovation that allows entrepreneurs to streamline their operations, reduce costs, and focus on delivering what customers truly value. By identifying and eliminating factors of limited value, entrepreneurs can create a more competitive and efficient business model that is better positioned to succeed in the marketplace.

THE IMPORTANCE OF IDENTIFYING FACTORS THAT CAN BE ELIMINATED

Identifying factors that are of limited to no real value to target customers is crucial for entrepreneurs because it enables them to streamline their resources and allocate them more effectively. In many cases, entrepreneurs can become preoccupied with delivering a range of features, products, or services to their target customers without fully understanding which ones are valued most by their customers. This can lead to wasted time, money, and effort on aspects that do not add any significant value to the customer experience or their overall satisfaction.

By identifying factors that are of limited to no real value to their target customers, entrepreneurs can prioritize their resources and focus on what really matters to their customers. They can then allocate their resources accordingly and deliver a more streamlined offering designed specifically to meet the needs of their target customers. By doing so, entrepreneurs can increase customer satisfaction, which can lead to greater loyalty, and ultimately more sales and revenue.

In addition, identifying and eliminating these factors can help entrepreneurs differentiate themselves from their competitors. This is because many of their competitors may be offering similar products or services, but with unnecessary features or elements that customers do not value. By focusing on what truly matters to their customers and streamlining their offerings accordingly, entrepreneurs can create a unique selling proposition that makes their offerings more attractive than those of their competitors. This can help them attract more customers, build a loyal customer base, and ultimately achieve greater success.

Identifying factors of limited to no real value to target customers is essential for entrepreneurs because it enables them to prioritize their resources, increase customer satisfaction, and differentiate themselves. By streamlining their offerings and focusing on what truly matters to their customers, entrepreneurs can create a more valuable and unique customer experience, leading to greater success in the marketplace.

FACTORS THAT CAN BE ELIMINATED

In value innovation, it's important to identify factors that are of limited or no value to customers and eliminate them to streamline the business and create a more efficient and effective value proposition. Here are some examples of factors that can be eliminated:

- **Unnecessary features:** In some cases, a product may have too many features that are not important to the customer. These features may drive up the cost of the product without adding much value. By eliminating these unnecessary features, the product can be streamlined and made more affordable.

- **Excessive packaging:** Customers may not see much value in excessive packaging, especially if it adds to the cost of the product. By reducing the amount of packaging or using more sustainable materials, a business can make their product more appealing to environmentally conscious customers.

- **Complex pricing structures:** Pricing structures that are overly complicated can be confusing to customers and may discourage them from making a purchase. By simplifying pricing and making it more transparent, a business can make it easier for customers to understand the value of their product.

- **Redundant processes:** In some cases, businesses may have processes in place that are redundant or not necessary. By identifying these inefficiencies and eliminating them, the business can save time and money and make operations more efficient.

- **Inefficient technologies:** Outdated or inefficient technologies can slow down a business and make it difficult to compete in the market. By upgrading to more modern and efficient technologies, a business can improve operations and provide a better customer experience.

By identifying and eliminating these types of factors, a business can create a more streamlined and effective value proposition that is more appealing to customers and more competitive in the market.

HOW APPLE ELIMINATED FACTORS

One example of a company that eliminated factors on a new product is Apple, Inc. with the launch of the first-generation iPhone in 2007. At the time, the mobile phone market was dominated by companies like Nokia, Blackberry, and Motorola. However, Apple's iPhone stood out as a game-changer in the industry, in large part because of the factors it eliminated.

Apple identified that many of the features on traditional mobile phones were of limited value to customers. Instead of trying to cram in as many features as possible, Apple chose to eliminate several features and prioritize others. For example, the iPhone did not have a physical keyboard, a common feature on mobile phones at the time. Instead, it featured a touch screen that allowed users to type and navigate the phone using gestures.

Additionally, the iPhone eliminated the need for a separate music player, like the iPod, by integrating a music player into the device. This eliminated the need for users to carry multiple devices and simplified the user experience.

Apple also eliminated the need for a stylus or other input device by introducing multi-touch technology, allowing users to interact with the device using only their fingers. This streamlined the user experience and eliminated the need for an additional accessory.

By eliminating features like a physical keyboard, separate music player, and stylus, Apple was able to create a product that was simple, intuitive, and easy to use. This approach resonated with customers and helped Apple to establish a foothold in the mobile phone market. The iPhone has since become one of the most successful consumer products of all time, with over two billion units sold worldwide.

THE BENEFITS OF ELIMINATING FACTORS

Eliminating factors can bring several benefits to the company and its customers. Some of these benefits are:

- **Cost Savings:** When a company eliminates certain features or services that are not valuable to the customers, it can reduce the cost of production, packaging, and marketing, leading to higher profit margins.
- **Increased Focus:** By eliminating certain features, the company can focus its resources on the more valuable aspects of the product, such as improving the quality of the remaining features or adding new features that customers find more valuable.

- **Improved Efficiency:** By eliminating unnecessary features or services, the company can streamline its production and delivery processes, resulting in faster, more efficient service to customers.

- **Improved Customer Experience:** Eliminating factors that are of limited value to customers can improve their overall experience with the product, as they can focus on the features and benefits that are most important to them.

- **Competitive Advantage:** By eliminating factors that are of limited value, the company can differentiate itself from competitors, providing a unique selling point that can attract more customers and increase its market share.

- **Simplified Decision-Making:** By removing unnecessary features, the company can simplify the decision-making process for customers, making it easier for them to understand and appreciate the product's value.

For example, Apple's decision to remove the headphone jack from its iPhones brought several benefits to both the company and its customers. The removal of the headphone jack reduced the cost of production and allowed the company to make other design changes that improved the user experience. Customers no longer had to carry a separate adapter for their headphones, and the new wireless AirPods provided a unique selling point for the iPhone, improving its competitive advantage. Additionally, the decision to eliminate the headphone jack simplified the decision-making process for customers, making it easier for them to appreciate the other features and benefits of the phone.

2. What to Reduce

By reducing certain factors, entrepreneurs can create cost savings for their company, which can be reinvested into other areas of the business, such as research and development or marketing. This can result in increased profits and greater success for the company.

Reducing factors can also help to make the product or service more accessible to a wider range of customers, particularly those who may have been deterred by a higher price point. This can lead to increased sales and revenue for the company, as well as increased customer satisfaction.

For example, a clothing company may decide to reduce the number of buttons on a shirt or remove unnecessary pockets to create a more streamlined, minimalist design. This would result in a reduction in production costs and a lower retail price for the customer while maintaining the same level of quality and style. This reduction in price may attract more customers who were previously deterred by the higher cost, leading to increased sales and revenue for the company.

In addition to cost savings and increased accessibility, reducing factors can also help to differentiate the product or service from competitors. By offering a product or service with fewer, more essential features, entrepreneurs can cater to customers who prioritize simplicity and functionality over unnecessary bells and whistles. This can create a unique selling point for the company.

Overall, reducing factors can be a valuable strategy for entrepreneurs seeking to create value innovation. By minimizing or eliminating non-essential features, entrepreneurs can reduce costs, increase accessibility, and differentiate their product or service from competitors, ultimately leading to increased success and company profitability.

THE IMPORTANCE OF FACTORS THAT CAN BE REDUCED

Identifying factors that can be reduced without significantly reducing the value delivered to customers is critical for entrepreneurs pursuing value innovation. In the context of the value curve, these are typically factors that are important to customers but don't necessarily need to be at their highest level to create value.

Reducing certain factors can be essential for entrepreneurs looking to achieve a competitive advantage. If a company can reduce costs or eliminate unnecessary features without negatively impacting the value provided to customers, it can offer a more attractive price point, making the product or service more accessible to a larger customer base. This can be especially important for startups that are entering crowded markets with established competitors.

For example, consider a company that produces high-end audio equipment. By reducing the number of inputs and outputs on its products, the company can lower costs and offer its products at a lower price point without sacrificing sound quality, which is the primary factor that customers care about. This allows the company to attract a larger customer base that may not be willing to pay the premium price for additional features that they don't necessarily need.

Reducing factors can also be important in situations where customers are overwhelmed with options. In these cases, reducing the number of options can improve the overall customer experience. For example, a restaurant that offers a simple menu with a limited number of high-quality options can stand out in a crowded market, making it easier for customers to make decisions.

Overall, reducing factors can benefit both the company and its customers. It allows the company to reduce costs and offer more attractive prices, while still delivering the same value to customers. At the same time, it can improve the overall customer experience by reducing decision fatigue and making it easier for customers to make purchase decisions.

FACTORS THAT CAN BE REDUCED

Factors that can be reduced in the context of value innovation can include various features, aspects of production, delivery, and customer service. Here are some examples:

- **Materials and Production Costs:** A company can look for ways to reduce the costs of raw materials, production methods, and logistics, without compromising the quality or functionality of the product. For example, a furniture manufacturer can use recycled or eco-friendly materials, optimize the use of space in the warehouse, and minimize waste to reduce costs and environmental impact.

- **Size and Complexity:** A product that is too big, heavy, or complex can be intimidating, inconvenient, and expensive to produce, transport, and maintain. A company can look for ways to simplify the design, packaging, and instructions, and make the product more user-friendly and accessible. For example, a consumer electronics company can make a compact, versatile device that combines multiple functions and requires minimal setup and maintenance.

- **Customer Support:** Providing extensive customer support, such as with call centers, manuals, and warranties, can be costly and time-consuming for a company and overwhelming or frustrating for the customer. A company can look for ways to reduce the need for customer support, such as by making the product more intuitive, reliable, and durable, or by providing online tutorials, troubleshooting guides, and self-service options. For example, a software company can make a user-friendly, bug-free program that requires minimal updates or user input and provides a knowledge base and forum for common issues and questions.

- **Delivery Time and Cost:** A company can look for ways to streamline the delivery process, such as by partnering with a logistics provider, optimizing routes and schedules, and reducing the packaging and handling time. For example, a food delivery service can use a network of local suppliers and drivers, prioritize orders based on proximity and volume, and use minimal packaging and utensils to reduce the delivery time and cost.

- **Special Features and Options:** A product that offers many options and features can be overwhelming and confusing for the customer, and expensive and complicated for the company. A company can look for ways to simplify and streamline the product by focusing on the essential features and eliminating or bundling the optional ones. For example, a car manufacturer can make a basic model with a few essential features, such as air conditioning and a radio, and offer a few packages of optional features, such as GPS and leather seats, rather than a long list of individual options.

HOW TESLA REDUCED FACTORS

When Tesla entered the automotive market in 2003, the electric vehicle industry faced significant challenges, including limited range, high costs, and inadequate charging infrastructure. Tesla recognized these barriers as opportunities for innovation and set out to revolutionize the industry.

Tesla identified key factors that needed to be reduced to overcome adoption barriers and accelerate the transition to electric vehicles:

- **Range Anxiety:** Range anxiety, the fear of running out of battery charge, was a significant concern for potential electric vehicle buyers. Tesla focused on improving battery technology, investing in research and development to create high-capacity lithium-ion batteries that could provide longer ranges. Their flagship Model S, introduced in 2012, boasted an industry-leading range of over 300 miles, significantly reducing range anxiety.

- **Cost:** The high cost of electric vehicles compared to traditional internal combustion engine vehicles was a major deterrent for many customers. Tesla embarked on a mission to reduce the cost of electric vehicles by vertically integrating their supply chain, developing in-house manufacturing capabilities, and scaling up production volumes. This allowed them to achieve economies of scale and gradually reduce the prices of their vehicles.

- **Charging Infrastructure:** The limited availability of charging stations was a critical barrier to electric vehicle adoption. Tesla took a bold step to address this challenge by deploying their proprietary Supercharger network. These high-speed charging stations were strategically located along major highways, enabling long-distance travel, and reducing charging time significantly. Tesla also pioneered the development of home charging solutions, making it convenient for customers to charge their vehicles overnight.

- **Design and Performance:** Electric vehicles were often perceived as lacking in design aesthetics and performance capabilities compared to their gasoline-powered counterparts. Tesla focused on creating sleek, attractive designs and high-performance electric vehicles that could compete with luxury gasoline vehicles. Their emphasis on innovation and cutting-edge technology helped overcome the perception that electric vehicles were inferior in terms of style and performance.

Through their relentless pursuit of reducing factors such as range anxiety, cost, charging infrastructure limitations, and design/performance concerns, Tesla has played a pivotal role in transforming the electric vehicle industry. Their visionary approach, technological innovation, and commitment to sustainable transportation have not only revolutionized the market but have also paved the way for the widespread adoption of electric vehicles worldwide. Tesla's success serves as an inspiration for other companies to address challenges head-on and drive the transition towards a sustainable future.

Overall, reducing factors can help companies create a more efficient, focused, and differentiated product that delivers real value to customers. It can also lead to cost savings, increased customer satisfaction, and a competitive advantage in the market.

3. What to Raise

Raising factors involves evaluating the value curve to identify the most critical factors to the customer and then increasing those factors to deliver additional value to the customer. The goal is to improve the customer's experience and enhance the perceived value of the product or service without significantly increasing the cost.

Entrepreneurs can raise factors in various ways, including increasing the quality of the product, adding features, improving the product's performance, enhancing customer service, and creating a better customer experience. For instance, a coffee shop may raise its factors by offering better quality coffee, expanding the menu to include more varieties, and providing free Wi-Fi services, comfortable seating, and a cozy ambiance.

Raising factors involves understanding customer needs and preferences and incorporating them into the product development process. This approach can help entrepreneurs differentiate their products or services from those of competitors, build brand loyalty, and capture a larger market share.

In summary, raising factors is a value innovation strategy that entrepreneurs use to improve the perceived value of their products or services. By increasing critical factors that meet the customer's needs and demands, entrepreneurs can create unique and innovative products that attract more customers and drive business growth.

IMPORTANCE OF IDENTIFYING FACTORS THAT CAN BE RAISED

Identifying factors that can be raised to increase the value delivered to customers is an important aspect of value innovation for entrepreneurs. Raising factors can lead to increased satisfaction and loyalty among customers, which in turn can lead to increased sales and revenue for the company. By identifying and raising factors that are important to customers, entrepreneurs can create a competitive advantage that sets them apart from their competitors.

One of the key benefits of identifying factors that can be raised is that it allows entrepreneurs to differentiate their products or services from those of their competitors. By offering superior value in certain areas, they can attract customers who are looking for those specific features or benefits. This can also help to create a strong brand image and reputation, which can further drive customer loyalty and attract new customers.

Another benefit of identifying factors that can be raised is that it can lead to increased profitability for the company. By identifying factors that are important to customers, entrepreneurs can invest in improving those areas, resulting in higher prices and margins. This can help offset any costs associated with the improvements and increase the overall profitability of the company.

Furthermore, identifying factors that can be raised can help entrepreneurs keep pace with changing customer needs and preferences. As the market and industry evolve, customer demands may change, and entrepreneurs who anticipate and respond to these changes by raising the right factors can gain a competitive advantage.

In summary, identifying factors that can be raised is an important part of value innovation for entrepreneurs. By raising the right factors, they can differentiate their products or services, create a strong brand image, increase profitability, and stay ahead of changing customer needs and preferences.

FACTORS THAT CAN BE RAISED

Factors that can be raised to increase the value delivered to customers can vary depending on the product or service being offered, the industry, and the target market. However, some examples of factors that can be raised to provide greater value to customers include:

- **Quality:** Improving the quality of a product or service is one way to increase the value delivered to customers. For example, a restaurant may source higher quality ingredients to improve the taste and overall experience for diners.

- **Convenience:** Making a product or service more convenient for customers can increase its perceived value. For example, a grocery store offering online ordering and delivery can save customers time and effort.

- **Customization:** Providing customers with the ability to customize a product or service to meet their individual needs or preferences can increase its value. For example, a clothing retailer may offer custom sizing options to ensure a better fit for customers.

- **Innovation:** Introducing new and innovative features or technology can increase the value of a product or service. For example, a phone manufacturer may introduce new camera features to improve the quality of photos.

- **Customer Service:** Providing exceptional customer service can increase the perceived value of a product or service. For example, a hotel may offer personalized recommendations and 24/7 concierge service to enhance the guest experience.
- **Branding:** Investing in branding and marketing efforts can increase the perceived value of a product or service. For example, a luxury car manufacturer may focus on the prestige and exclusivity associated with its brand to increase its value to customers.

By identifying factors that can be raised to increase the value delivered to customers, companies can differentiate themselves in the market, create a unique value proposition, and drive sales and customer loyalty.

How Nike Raised Factors

One example of a company that raised factors on a new product is Nike with their Flywire technology. Nike's Flywire technology is a unique method of construction that uses high-strength threads to support the foot. This technology reduces the weight of the shoe without sacrificing beneficial features. Nike's aim was to make shoes lighter and more comfortable without reducing their performance or support. Nike identified that shoe weight is a significant factor for athletes and reducing it can improve performance.

To develop the Flywire technology, Nike used a new material and construction technique that eliminated unnecessary weight from the shoe. By removing material in non-essential areas and using high-strength threads to support the foot, Nike was able to create a shoe that was both lightweight and supportive. The resulting product was a new line of shoes that were much lighter and more comfortable than the competition, providing a significant competitive advantage.

Flywire technology was first introduced in Nike's basketball shoes and later expanded to other types of shoes, including running and training shoes. Nike's Flywire technology has become a key selling point for its shoes and has been widely adopted by other shoe manufacturers. By raising the factor of shoe weight, Nike was able to create a new market space and differentiate itself from its competitors.

Nike's Flywire technology provides several benefits to both the company and its customers. For Nike, it has helped to differentiate its shoes from competitors and has become a key selling point. By raising the factor of shoe weight, Nike was able to develop a new market space that it could dominate. Customers benefit from the technology by having access to shoes that are lighter and more comfortable, providing improved performance and reducing fatigue during long workouts.

BENEFITS OF RAISING FACTORS

Raising factors in the context of value innovation can offer several benefits to the company and its customers. Some of these benefits include:

- **Increased Customer Satisfaction:** By raising factors, a company can increase the value delivered to its customers. This can lead to higher levels of customer satisfaction and loyalty.
- **Increased Brand Recognition:** Companies that can differentiate themselves from their competitors through the factors they raise can build a stronger brand. This can lead to increased recognition and customer preference.
- **Competitive Advantage:** Raising factors can give a company a competitive advantage over its rivals. By offering a unique product or service that delivers more value to customers, a company can set itself apart and capture a larger market share.

- **Improved Profitability:** By raising factors, a company can charge a premium price for its products or services. This can lead to increased profitability and financial performance.

- **Innovation Leadership:** By introducing new, innovative factors to the market, a company can establish itself as a leader in its industry. This can help the company attract top talent, investors, and partnerships.

- **Customer Evangelism:** When a company raises factors that customers highly value, customers are likely to become advocates for the brand. This can lead to increased word-of-mouth marketing and customer acquisition.

Raising factors is a powerful way for a company to increase the value it delivers to customers while setting distinguishing itself from competitors. By focusing on the factors that customers value most, a company can create a differentiated product or service that drives customer satisfaction, loyalty, and financial performance.

4. What to Create

Creating new factors requires companies to approach product development from a different perspective, often by identifying unmet customer needs and developing new products or services that address those needs. This can involve exploring entirely new technologies or developing new business models that have not been previously used in the industry.

Creating in the context of value innovation involves understanding the current limitations of existing products or services and finding ways to overcome those limitations with new and innovative ideas. This requires a deep understanding of the needs and preferences of the target customer segment, as well as an ability to identify emerging trends and anticipate future market needs.

Creating something new can be a risky strategy, as it involves a significant investment in research and development, and there is always the possibility that the new product or service may not be successful in the market. However, companies that successfully create entirely new factors can often reap significant rewards, as they can establish themselves as market leaders and capture a significant market share.

Overall, creating new factors is a crucial part of value innovation and can be a powerful tool for companies looking to differentiate themselves and create uncontested market space.

IMPORTANCE OF IDENTIFYING NEW FACTORS

In the context of value innovation, creating new factors means developing unique features not offered by any existing products or services in the market. This is a crucial aspect of value innovation as it allows companies to differentiate their offerings and create new demand by catering to previously untapped customer needs.

Identifying new factors that can be created is important for companies as it allows them to explore new business opportunities and establish themselves as market leaders. Companies that are successful in identifying and creating new factors can significantly increase their revenue and profitability by attracting a new customer base.

Furthermore, creating new factors helps companies to stay ahead of the competition by offering unique value propositions to their customers. This, in turn, leads to brand loyalty and the development of a strong customer base that can act as brand advocates for the company. By creating new factors, companies can also establish a strong barrier to entry for potential competitors, which can help them maintain their market position in the long run.

Another benefit of creating new factors is that it allows companies to engage in continuous innovation, which is necessary in today's rapidly evolving business environment. By continuously creating new features, companies can stay relevant and adapt to changing market trends and customer preferences.

For customers, the creation of new factors means they have access to new and innovative products or services that can enhance their quality of life. It allows them to experience something different, which can help them solve their problems and address their needs in a better way.

In summary, identifying new factors that can be created is important for companies as it allows them to differentiate their offerings, attract new customers, and establish a strong market position. It also allows companies to engage in continuous innovation, which is necessary in today's business environment and provides customers access to new and innovative products or services.

FACTORS THAT CAN BE CREATED

Creating new factors is an essential part of value innovation that allows companies to differentiate themselves from competitors and deliver unique value to customers. Here are a few examples of factors that companies can create:

- **New Features or Functionalities:** Companies can create new features or functionalities that are not currently available in the market. For example, Tesla created the "Autopilot" feature for its electric cars, allowing hands-free driving on highways.
- **Unique Design Elements:** Companies can create unique design elements that make their products stand out. For example, Dyson created a unique bladeless design for its fans and air purifiers, which has become a hallmark of the brand.

- **Personalization and Customization:** Companies can create personalized or customizable products that allow customers to tailor the product to their specific needs or preferences. For example, Nike created the NikeID platform, which allows customers to design their own shoes and apparel.

- **New Business Models:** Companies can create new business models that disrupt the existing market. For example, Netflix created a subscription-based model for streaming movies and TV shows, which has since become the industry standard.

- **Innovative Materials:** Companies can create innovative materials that provide unique properties or benefits. For example, Gore-Tex created a waterproof and breathable fabric that has become widely used in outdoor apparel.

- **New distribution Channels:** Companies can create new distribution channels that make their products more accessible or convenient for customers. For example, Warby Parker created an online platform for ordering eyeglasses, which allows customers to try on glasses at home and get a prescription without visiting a physical store.

- **Environmental Sustainability:** Companies can create environmentally sustainable products or production processes that are more eco-friendly than current alternatives. For example, Patagonia has created a line of outdoor apparel made from recycled materials and has implemented sustainable production practices in its factories.

These are just a few examples of the types of factors that companies can create to deliver value innovation. By identifying new factors that are not currently available in the market, companies can create new demand and carve out a unique position for themselves in the industry.

HOW BEYOND MEAT CREATED NEW FACTORS

Beyond Meat is a leading American food company founded by Ethan Brown in 2009 with a mission to create plant-based meat alternatives that replicate the taste, texture, and experience of animal-based meat products. By focusing on creating innovative plant-based alternatives, Beyond Meat aims to address environmental and health concerns while providing consumers with sustainable and delicious food options.

The meat industry has long been associated with environmental issues, including deforestation, greenhouse gas emissions, and water pollution. Beyond Meat recognized the need to offer consumers an alternative that could deliver the taste and experience of animal-based meat while reducing the environmental impact.

Beyond Meat's approach involves creating plant-based meat alternatives that closely mimic the taste, texture, and appearance of traditional meat products. By combining innovative food science, cutting-edge technology, and plant-based ingredients, the company has developed a range of products that cater to different consumer preferences and dietary needs.

- **Beyond Burger:** Beyond Meat's flagship product, the Beyond Burger, is designed to replicate the taste and texture of a traditional beef burger. It is made from a blend of plant-based ingredients, such as peas, mung beans, and rice protein, with beet juice for a meat-like red color. The Beyond Burger has been praised for its resemblance to beef and its ability to satisfy the cravings of meat lovers.

288

- **Beyond Sausage:** Beyond Meat expanded its product line to include plant-based sausages that closely resemble traditional pork sausages. The Beyond Sausage is made from a blend of plant proteins, including peas, fava beans, and rice, creating a juicy and flavorful alternative to animal-based sausages.

- **Beyond Ground:** Recognizing the versatility of ground meat in various recipes, Beyond Meat developed Beyond Ground, a plant-based alternative to ground beef. Beyond Ground can be used as a replacement in recipes such as tacos, pasta dishes, and chili, offering a convenient and sustainable option for consumers.

Beyond Meat's focus on creating plant-based meat alternatives has yielded significant impact and results:

- **Sustainability:** By using plant-based ingredients, Beyond Meat reduces the environmental impact associated with traditional meat production. Their products require fewer natural resources and produce fewer greenhouse gas emissions than animal-based alternatives.

- **Health Benefits:** Beyond Meat's products are cholesterol-free, lower in saturated fat, and contain no antibiotics or hormones, making them a healthier choice for consumers concerned about their dietary health.

- **Market Penetration:** Beyond Meat's success in creating plant-based meat alternatives has allowed the company to penetrate both retail and food service channels globally. Their products are available in supermarkets, restaurants, and fast-food chains, expanding accessibility and choice for consumers.

Beyond Meat's commitment to creating plant-based meat alternatives has revolutionized the food industry and changed perceptions about plant-based eating. By focusing on taste, texture, and sustainability, the company has successfully created products that cater to the evolving consumer demand for sustainable and healthier food options. Beyond Meat's success serves as a testament to the potential of creating innovative and delicious plant-based alternatives, providing consumers with choices that align with their values and contribute to a more sustainable future.

BENEFITS OF CREATING FACTORS

Creating new factors can deliver significant benefits for both the company and its customers. Some of these benefits include:

- **Competitive Advantage:** By creating new factors that set their product or service apart, a company can gain a competitive advantage in the market. This can help the company to stand out from its competitors and attract new customers.

- **Increased Customer Satisfaction:** Creating new factors that meet the needs and preferences of customers can lead to higher levels of customer satisfaction. This can help to build customer loyalty and lead to repeat business.

- **Increased Profitability:** New factors that add value to a product or service can justify a higher price point, leading to increased profitability for the company. Additionally, the company may be able to reduce costs by eliminating or reducing factors that are not valuable to customers.

- **Innovation Culture:** Encouraging and rewarding employees for identifying and creating new factors can foster an innovative culture within the company. This can help the company stay ahead of its competitors and adapt to changing market conditions.

- **Brand Recognition:** Creating new factors that are unique and valuable can help build brand recognition and differentiate the company from its competitors. This can help the company build a strong reputation and increase its market share.

Overall, creating new factors can be a powerful tool for companies looking to stand out and deliver value to their customers. By identifying and implementing new factors, companies can gain a competitive advantage, increase customer satisfaction and loyalty, and improve profitability. Additionally, the process of creating new factors can foster an innovative culture within the company and build a strong brand reputation in the market.

HOW TO DELIVER VALUE INNOVATION

The four questions in the value innovation framework comprise a powerful tool for delivering value innovation. These questions are:

- What to eliminate?
- What to reduce?
- What to raise?
- What to create?

To use these questions effectively, a company needs to follow these steps:

1. **Identify the Value Proposition:** The company should identify its current value proposition and determine how it can be improved. The value proposition should be clearly defined, and the company should have a thorough understanding of its customers' needs and preferences.

2. **Analyze the Market:** The company should analyze the current market trends and identify the areas where there is a gap. It should also analyze its competitors' offerings and determine what they are missing.

3. **Use the Four Questions:** Once the company has identified its value proposition and analyzed the market, it should use the four questions to develop its value innovation strategy. For example, it could identify factors that are of limited value to customers and eliminate them. It could reduce the price of its offering or the time it takes to deliver the product. It could raise the quality of its product or service or the level of customer service. It could create a new feature or functionality that its competitors do not offer.

4. **Develop the Offering:** The company should then develop the offering based on the answers to the four questions. The offering should be designed to meet the needs of the target customers and deliver superior value.

5. **Test and Refine:** The company should test the offering with its target customers and refine it based on their feedback. This will help to ensure that the offering is meeting the customers' needs and delivering value.

6. **Launch and Market:** Once the offering has been developed and refined, the company should launch it and market it to its target customers. The marketing campaign should be designed to highlight the unique value proposition of the offering and differentiate it from the competitors' offerings.

By using the above steps and the four questions in the value innovation framework, a company can deliver value innovation and create a new market space that is uncontested by its competitors.

IMPORTANCE OF ALIGNING THE WHOLE SYSTEM OF BENEFITS, PRICE, AND COST

When delivering value innovation, it is essential to align the entire system of benefits, price, and cost to ensure a successful outcome for the company and its customers.

The benefits that a company offers are the perceived advantages that a product or service provides to customers. These benefits are what customers are willing to pay for, and they form the basis for creating value innovation. The price that a company charges for its products or services should reflect the benefits provided to customers. The price must be set at a level that customers are willing to pay, and it must be competitive with other offerings in the market.

The cost is the amount of money a company incurs to deliver its products or services. To ensure profitability, the cost must be less than the price charged to customers. This can be achieved by reducing the cost of production, improving efficiency, or negotiating better deals with suppliers.

Aligning the system of benefits, price, and cost is essential for several reasons. First, it ensures that the company is providing value to customers, which is essential for long-term success. If customers do not see the benefits of a product or service, they will not purchase it, and the company will not be successful. Second, aligning the system ensures that the price charged for the product or service is competitive with other offerings in the market. If the price is too high, customers will not purchase the product, and if it is too low, the company will not be profitable. Finally, aligning the system ensures that the cost of delivering the product or service is manageable and the company can make a profit.

For example, a company may create a new product that offers several benefits to customers, such as being more durable, having more features, and being easier to use. However, if the price is too high, customers may not be willing to pay for these benefits. Conversely, if the price is too low, the company may not be able to cover the cost of production and will not be profitable. By aligning the system of benefits, price, and cost, the company can ensure that the new product is successful in the market.

In conclusion, aligning the system of benefits, price, and cost is crucial for delivering value innovation. It ensures that the company provides value to customers, the price charged is competitive, and the cost of production is manageable. This alignment is essential for the long-term success of the company and the satisfaction of its customers.

REMEMBER

The chapter on value innovation introduces the concept of creating new value in the market by simultaneously pursuing differentiation and low cost. The traditional approach of competing on price or features is unsustainable and results in "bloody competition" in overcrowded marketplaces. A new approach is creating a blue ocean, which is a new market space where the competition is irrelevant, and the rules of the game are yet to be established. This is achieved by identifying and addressing the factors of value that matter to customers and eliminating, reducing, raising, or creating new factors to deliver a unique and compelling value proposition.

The process of delivering value innovation involves four key questions, which are used to help companies understand what factors of value matter to their customers and how they can deliver them in a way that is differentiated and low cost. These questions are:

- What factors of value should be eliminated that the industry has long competed on?
- What factors of value should be reduced well below the industry's standard?
- What factors of value should be raised well above the industry's standard?
- What factors of value should be created that the industry has never offered?

Recognize the importance of aligning the whole system of benefits, price, and cost to deliver value innovation. This involves creating a compelling value proposition that appeals to customers while achieving low cost and generating profit for the company. A company can align its whole system by focusing on three key factors: buyer utility, price, and cost.

In summary, value innovation is about creating a new market space that is free from competition by identifying and addressing the factors of value that matter to customers. This is achieved by eliminating, reducing, raising, or creating new factors to deliver a unique and compelling value proposition. The key to delivering value innovation is to align the whole system of benefits, price, and cost. The chapter offers practical advice and examples for entrepreneurs and business leaders who seek to create new market space and deliver value innovation.

FINAL THOUGHTS ON THE ROLE OF VALUE INNOVATION IN ENTREPRENEURSHIP

Value innovation is a crucial concept in entrepreneurship that helps companies to stand out in highly competitive markets. By identifying and delivering superior value to customers, entrepreneurs can create new demand and capture untapped markets. By focusing on the four key questions of what to eliminate, reduce, raise, and create, entrepreneurs can deliver value innovation that differentiates their products and services from competitors. Moreover, it is important to align the entire system of benefits, price, and cost to ensure that the value is delivered in a sustainable and profitable way. Value innovation is about creating new and uncontested market space where entrepreneurs can thrive and create long-term value for their customers and stakeholders. By applying these principles, entrepreneurs can transform their businesses and achieve success in today's rapidly changing business landscape.

16. Opportunity Identification

Opportunities are usually disguised as hard work,
so most people don't recognize them.

Ann Landers
Advice Columnist and Entrepreneur

Entrepreneurial opportunities become real when you have a solution that leverages your advantages to solve an important problem for customers. This chapter examines how to translate the approaches and tools of this book to act on real entrepreneurial opportunities. The key elements of opportunity identification are *defining the problem, crafting a competitive solution, building your advantage,* and *forming the right team.*

The Opportunity Analysis Canvas

Emphasis on "Opportunity Identification"

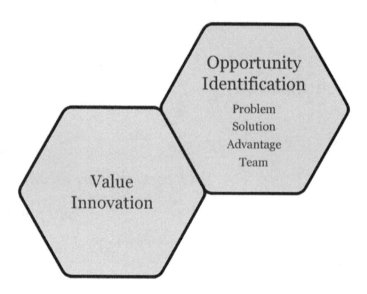

Identifying real entrepreneurial opportunities is critical for entrepreneurs because it ensures they are solving a real problem and meeting a genuine need. The process of opportunity identification involves identifying gaps in the market, understanding customer needs, and finding ways to create value for the customer.

Without identifying a real opportunity, entrepreneurs risk investing significant time and resources in developing a product or service that may not have a market or meet customer needs. This can lead to failure and wasted resources, both in terms of time and money.

Identifying real entrepreneurial opportunities also allows entrepreneurs to rise above their competitors and create a unique value proposition. By focusing on solving a specific problem or meeting a specific need, entrepreneurs can develop a product or service that is better than what is currently available on the market. This can lead to increased customer satisfaction and loyalty, and ultimately, increased profitability.

In addition, identifying real entrepreneurial opportunities can also help entrepreneurs attract investors and partners. By demonstrating that there is a real need in the market and a strong demand for their product or service, entrepreneurs can make a compelling case to potential investors and partners.

Finally, identifying real entrepreneurial opportunities allows entrepreneurs to align their passion with a meaningful purpose. Many entrepreneurs start their ventures with a strong desire to make a positive impact or solve a specific problem. By identifying a real opportunity, entrepreneurs can channel their passion and energy into something that has the potential to create real value for their customers and the world.

Identifying real entrepreneurial opportunities is essential for the success of any new venture. It ensures that entrepreneurs are creating a product or service that meets a real need, creates value for customers, and has the potential to be profitable and impactful.

KEY ELEMENTS OF OPPORTUNITY IDENTIFICATION

Opportunity identification is a critical process in entrepreneurship involving identifying and evaluating potential business opportunities that can lead to the creation of a successful venture. This chapter discusses the key elements of opportunity identification and how entrepreneurs can apply them to identify and act on real entrepreneurial opportunities. The key elements of opportunity identification are:

- **Defining the Problem:** The first step in identifying entrepreneurial opportunities is to define a problem that needs to be solved. Entrepreneurs should focus on understanding customers' pain points and identifying problems that have not been solved or have been poorly solved by existing solutions. The problem should be significant enough to provide a market opportunity for a new solution.

- **Crafting a Competitive Solution:** After identifying a problem, entrepreneurs need to craft a competitive solution that addresses the problem in a unique and compelling way. This requires creativity and a deep understanding of the problem and its underlying causes. Entrepreneurs should focus on developing solutions that provide significant value to customers and differentiate themselves from existing solutions.

- **Building Your Advantage:** To succeed in a competitive marketplace, entrepreneurs need to build a competitive advantage that allows them to create and capture value. This may involve leveraging unique skills, capabilities, or resources to create a distinctive value proposition. Entrepreneurs should focus on building a sustainable competitive advantage that can be defended against competitors.

- **Forming the Right Team:** The success of an entrepreneurial venture depends on the team behind it. Entrepreneurs should focus on building a team that has the necessary skills, experience, and resources to execute on the opportunity. This includes identifying co-founders, key employees, advisors, and investors who can help bring the opportunity to fruition.

By focusing on these key elements, entrepreneurs can identify and act on real entrepreneurial opportunities that have the potential to create significant value for customers and the business. The process of opportunity identification is an iterative one, and entrepreneurs should be prepared to refine and adapt their approach as they learn more about the problem, the market, and the competitive landscape.

Defining the Problem

For entrepreneurs, identifying and understanding the problem is an essential part of opportunity identification. Without a clear understanding of the problem, it is difficult to create a competitive and effective solution that meets customer needs.

Identifying and understanding the problem can be a challenging task for entrepreneurs, because it requires a deep understanding of the market, industry, and customer needs. This involves gathering data, conducting market research, and analyzing customer feedback to identify pain points and areas where current solutions are lacking. By understanding the problem, entrepreneurs can identify unmet customer needs and develop solutions that address those needs more effectively.

Furthermore, identifying and understanding the problem is crucial for creating a solution that has a market demand. By identifying a real problem, entrepreneurs can create a product or service that fills a gap in the market and provides a better solution to existing alternatives. This not only ensures that there is a demand for the solution but also sets the foundation for a successful business.

In addition, understanding the problem can also help entrepreneurs to differentiate their solution from competitors. By identifying areas where current solutions are lacking, entrepreneurs can develop a solution that offers a unique value proposition and sets themselves apart from competitors. This can help create a competitive advantage and increase the likelihood of success.

Overall, identifying and understanding the problem is a critical element of opportunity identification for entrepreneurs. By doing so, entrepreneurs can create a solution that meets customer needs, has a market demand, and offers a unique value proposition that helps them stand out from the competition.

METHODS FOR IDENTIFYING AND EVALUATING PROBLEMS

Identifying and evaluating problems that can be the basis for a new startup company is crucial for entrepreneurs who seek to create successful businesses. In this context, entrepreneurs need to consider various methods for identifying and evaluating problems to ensure they can create products or services that truly meet the needs of the market.

One method for identifying problems is by conducting market research. This method involves gathering data on the target market, such as customer preferences, buying behavior, and industry trends. By understanding the needs and wants of potential customers, entrepreneurs can develop innovative products or services that solve real problems. Market research can be conducted through surveys, focus groups, or online analytics tools.

Another method for identifying problems is by looking at existing industries and finding inefficiencies or areas where there is a lack of competition. This method is known as gap analysis, and it can help entrepreneurs find areas where they can offer a unique solution. For example, an entrepreneur might identify a gap in the market for eco-friendly cleaning products and develop a line of all-natural cleaning solutions that meet this need.

Once entrepreneurs have identified potential problems, they need to evaluate them to determine their viability. One method for evaluating problems is by using a scoring model that considers factors such as the size of the market, the level of competition, and the potential profitability of the solution. This helps entrepreneurs prioritize the problems that have the most potential for success.

Another method for evaluating problems is by creating a minimum viable product (MVP). An MVP is a basic version of the product or service that can be tested with early adopters to determine if there is a demand for the solution. By testing the MVP, entrepreneurs can gather feedback and adjust ensure that the final product meets the needs of the market.

In summary, identifying and evaluating problems that can be the basis for a new startup company is crucial for entrepreneurs. By conducting market research, performing gap analysis, using scoring models, and creating MVPs, entrepreneurs can ensure that they develop products or services that truly meet the needs of the market and have the potential for success.

TECHNIQUES FOR RESEARCHING AND GATHERING DATA TO DEFINE THE PROBLEM

Defining the problem is a crucial step in identifying entrepreneurial opportunities. Gathering and researching data can help entrepreneurs define and refine the problem, which can lead to the creation of a more effective solution. Here are some techniques for researching and gathering data to define the problem:

- **Conduct Market Research:** Market research can help entrepreneurs understand their target customers, their needs and pain points, and what solutions are currently available in the market. It can be done through surveys, focus groups, and other market research techniques.
- **Use Social Media:** Social media platforms can be a great source of information for entrepreneurs. They can use social media to gather feedback, learn about customer preferences, and identify trends.
- **Talk to Experts:** Experts in the industry can provide valuable insights and help entrepreneurs understand the problem better. They can be industry leaders, academics, or consultants.

- **Analyze Existing Data:** Entrepreneurs can use existing data such as industry reports, customer feedback, and competitor analysis to identify and define the problem. This data can be obtained from various sources such as industry associations, government websites, and online databases.

- **Conduct Experiments:** Experiments can help entrepreneurs validate assumptions and test hypotheses. They can conduct experiments to test the viability of a solution and get feedback from potential customers.

- **Observe Customers:** Observing customers in their natural environment can provide valuable insights into their behavior, preferences, and pain points. This can be done through ethnographic research or by shadowing customers.

These techniques can help entrepreneurs gather data and insights that can help them define the problem and create a more effective solution. It's important to use a combination of these techniques to get a more comprehensive view of the problem and the potential solution.

HOW BUMBLE DEFINED THE PROBLEM

One entrepreneur who identified a problem and created a new company to address it is Whitney Wolfe Herd, the founder and CEO of Bumble, a dating app that empowers women to make the first move.

Before founding Bumble in 2014, Wolfe Herd co-founded Tinder, another popular dating app. However, she left the company in 2014 due to sexual harassment and discrimination by her co-founders. She then identified a problem in the dating app market: women often received unsolicited messages and unwanted attention from men, which made them uncomfortable and discouraged them from using apps.

To address this problem, Wolfe Herd founded Bumble, which only allows women to initiate conversations with their matches. This gives women control over the conversation and helps them avoid unwanted attention. The app has since expanded to include features like Bumble BFF, which helps people find friends, and Bumble Bizz, which helps people network and find business connections.

Wolfe Herd's focus on solving a problem and empowering women has paid off. Bumble went public in February 2021 and has a market capitalization of around $7 billion. Wolfe Herd is also the youngest woman to take a company public in the United States.

Through her focus on identifying a problem and addressing it with a unique solution, Wolfe Herd has created a successful and socially impactful company. She has also become a role model for women in tech and entrepreneurship, advocating for gender equality and supporting other women-led businesses through her investment fund, Bumble Fund.

Crafting a Competitive Solution

A competitive solution that meets customer needs is essential for the success of any new venture. It is not enough to identify a problem and develop a product or service that addresses the issue. The product or service needs to be competitive in the market and able to meet the needs of the target customer.

The importance of a competitive solution lies in the fact that there are likely to be other companies and products that are trying to solve the same problem. The success of a new venture will depend on how well it can compete with these other solutions. Customers will choose the solution that best meets their needs, and if a new venture cannot compete, it will not succeed.

A competitive solution is unique and provides value not offered by other solutions in the market. This can be achieved by creating a differentiated product or service that meets a customer's need in a better or more efficient way than the competition. Entrepreneurs must also consider the pricing of the product or service, as it must be competitive with other solutions in the market.

To develop a competitive solution, entrepreneurs must conduct market research to understand the needs of the target customer and the competition. This information can be used to identify gaps in the market where a new solution can provide value.

Another way to ensure a competitive solution is to continuously iterate and improve the product or service based on customer feedback. This allows the new venture to stay ahead of the competition by continuing to provide a solution that meets the changing needs of the customer.

In summary, the importance of a competitive solution is to ensure the success of a new venture by meeting the needs of the customer in a unique and valuable way. Entrepreneurs must conduct market research, develop a unique solution, and continuously iterate and improve the product or service to stay ahead of the competition.

Techniques for Idea Generation and Evaluation

Idea generation and evaluation are essential for entrepreneurial success. The process requires examining existing products, identifying areas that need improvement or where there is a gap in the market, and creating a competitive solution that meets customer needs. One effective way to generate ideas is by examining competing products. Here are some techniques for idea generation and evaluation with an emphasis on examining competing products:

- **Analyze Competing Products:** Entrepreneurs need to examine competing products to identify areas of improvement or gaps in the market. This analysis helps entrepreneurs generate ideas for new products that offer better value to customers.

- **Create a Mind Map:** Mind mapping is a technique that can be used to generate and organize ideas. It involves creating a visual diagram that shows the relationships between different ideas.

- **Brainstorming Sessions:** Brainstorming is a popular technique for generating new ideas. The process involves a group of people coming together to share ideas and bounce ideas off one another.

- **Conduct Customer Research:** Customer research is a critical step in the idea generation process. Entrepreneurs need to understand their target customers' needs, preferences, and pain points to develop products that meet their needs.

- **SWOT Analysis:** A SWOT analysis is a framework used to evaluate the strengths, weaknesses, opportunities, and threats of a product or company. Entrepreneurs can use this technique to evaluate their competing products and generate ideas for new products that capitalize on the opportunities.

- **Minimum Viable Product:** A minimum viable product (MVP) is a product with enough features to satisfy early customers and provide feedback for future product development. Entrepreneurs can create an MVP to test the viability of their new product idea.

In conclusion, entrepreneurs must use a combination of techniques to generate and evaluate ideas for new products. Examining competing products is a crucial step in this process, as it helps entrepreneurs identify areas for improvement or gaps in the market. Entrepreneurs need to prioritize customer research, create a mind map, conduct brainstorming sessions, use SWOT analysis, and build a minimum viable product to develop a competitive solution that meets customer needs.

TECHNIQUES FOR SCREENING, TESTING, AND REFINING SOLUTIONS

Screening, testing, and refining solutions are critical steps for any entrepreneur who wants to bring a new product to market. The screening process helps identify the most promising solutions and eliminates the weaker ones. The testing process evaluates how well the solution meets customer needs, and the refining process helps to optimize the solution for the target market.

To screen solutions, entrepreneurs can use various techniques such as creating a checklist of key features that the solution should have, conducting SWOT analysis, or creating a decision matrix that compares the strengths and weaknesses of each solution. By doing this, entrepreneurs can identify the most promising solution that is most likely to meet the customer's needs.

Once the most promising solution has been identified, the next step is to test it. Testing helps to identify any potential flaws or weaknesses in the solution before it is released to the market. One way to test a solution is to create a prototype or a minimum viable product (MVP) that can be tested by a select group of customers. The feedback from these tests can be used to refine the solution and make it better suited to the needs of the target market.

Refining a solution is an iterative process that involves making changes to the solution based on customer feedback. Entrepreneurs can use various techniques such as surveys, focus groups, and A/B testing to gather feedback from customers. This feedback can be used to refine the solution and make it more effective and appealing to the target market.

In summary, screening, testing, and refining solutions are essential steps in the product development process. By using these techniques, entrepreneurs can ensure they develop a solution that meets the needs of the target market and is likely to be successful in the marketplace.

HOW EMBRACE INNOVATIONS CRAFTED A COMPETITIVE SOLUTION

One entrepreneur who crafted a competitive solution to address a problem is Jane Chen, the co-founder of Embrace Innovations. In 2010, Chen and her team identified a significant problem in developing countries where millions of premature and underweight babies were dying due to the lack of access to affordable incubators. Chen, who has a background in product design and development, realized that traditional incubators were expensive, bulky, and required a continuous power source, which made them impractical for use in many parts of the world. To address this problem, she and her team developed a low-cost, portable infant warmer that does not require electricity or continuous maintenance.

To craft a competitive solution, Chen and her team conducted extensive research on the problem, including talking to healthcare providers and families in developing countries to understand their needs and challenges. They also studied existing solutions, including traditional incubators and other low-cost alternatives, to identify their strengths and weaknesses.

Using this information, they began designing and prototyping their own solution, which involved a portable sleeping bag-like device that used phase change material to regulate the baby's temperature. The device was cost-effective, easy to use, and did not require electricity or continuous maintenance, making it ideal for use in developing countries.

Once they had a working prototype, Chen and her team began testing and refining the solution through partnerships with hospitals and clinics in developing countries. They gathered feedback from healthcare providers and families to make further improvements to the product and its user experience.

Today, Embrace Innovations has expanded its product line to include several other healthcare products, all focusing on providing affordable, accessible, and innovative solutions to improve healthcare in developing countries. The company has received numerous awards and recognition for its impact on global health and social entrepreneurship.

Chen's example illustrates the importance of identifying a problem and developing a competitive solution that meets customer needs through thorough research, prototyping, testing, and refining. Her success shows that with persistence and innovation, entrepreneurs can create impactful solutions that improve the lives of millions of people around the world.

Building a Competitive Advantage

Building competitive advantages is crucial to the success of any startup company. To stand out in a crowded market and gain a competitive edge, entrepreneurs need to identify and leverage their unique strengths to create a compelling value proposition for their customers. Here are some reasons why building competitive advantages is important:

- **Differentiation:** Competitive advantages enable a startup to differentiate itself from other businesses in the market, helping it to stand out and attract customers. This differentiation could come in the form of a unique product or service offering, a superior customer experience, or a combination of these and other factors.

- **Barriers to Entry:** Competitive advantages can create barriers to entry that make it difficult for new competitors to enter the market. This can help protect the startup's market share and provide a buffer against competition.

- **Pricing Power:** If a startup has a competitive advantage that provides unique value to customers, it can charge a premium for its products or services. This can lead to higher profit margins and increased revenue for the company.

- **Innovation:** Competitive advantages can provide the impetus for innovation, as companies seek to continuously improve their products and services to stay ahead of the competition.

- **Brand Recognition:** By building competitive advantages, a startup can develop a strong brand that is recognized and valued by customers. This can lead to increased customer loyalty, word-of-mouth referrals, and a positive reputation in the market.

To build competitive advantages, entrepreneurs need to identify their unique strengths and leverage them to create a compelling value proposition for their customers. This can involve a range of activities, from investing in research and development to creating strong relationships with suppliers and partners. By continuously refining and improving their competitive advantages, startups can gain an edge in the market and build a foundation for long-term success.

TECHNIQUES FOR IDENTIFYING AND DEVELOPING YOUR UNIQUE COMPETITIVE ADVANTAGES

Identifying and developing unique competitive advantages is crucial for the success of any business. Here are some techniques to help entrepreneurs identify and develop their unique competitive advantages:

- **Analyze Your Strengths and Weaknesses:** Begin by analyzing your own strengths and weaknesses. This will help you identify the areas where you excel and where you need improvement. Make a list of your strengths, skills, and talents.

- **Conduct Market Research:** Market research is essential to identifying your unique competitive advantage. Analyze your competitors' strengths and weaknesses and compare them to your own. Determine what your customers are looking for and how you can meet their needs better than your competitors.

- **Identify What Makes You Different:** Identify what makes you unique and what sets you apart from your competitors. Determine what you offer that your competitors do not. This could be your level of expertise, your quality of service, your product features, or even your brand personality.

- **Build on Your Strengths:** Once you have identified your unique advantages, focus on building on them. If you excel in customer service, for example, develop strategies to improve and enhance the customer experience.

- **Develop a Unique Brand Identity:** Your brand identity is what sets you apart from your competitors. Develop a unique brand identity that reflects your strengths and competitive advantages. This will help you stand out in the market and attract customers.

- **Keep Innovating:** Your competitive advantages can become less effective over time if you don't continue to innovate. Continuously look for ways to improve and enhance your products or services to maintain your competitive edge.

In summary, entrepreneurs can identify and develop unique competitive advantages by analyzing their strengths and weaknesses, conducting market research, identifying what sets them apart, building on their strengths, developing a unique brand identity, and continuously innovating. By leveraging their unique advantages, entrepreneurs can create a sustainable competitive advantage and better meet the needs of their customers.

BUILDING A COMPETITIVE ADVANTAGE AT QUALTRICS

One example of an entrepreneur who built a competitive advantage to create a new product and company is Ryan Smith, the founder of Qualtrics, a software company that specializes in survey research and customer experience management.

Smith's unique competitive advantage came from his expertise in survey research and his ability to translate that knowledge into a user-friendly software platform. He recognized that traditional survey methods were outdated and inefficient and saw an opportunity to develop a more efficient and effective solution. He leveraged his background in survey research and understanding of business' needs to develop a software platform that could help companies gather and analyze customer feedback quickly and easily.

To build his competitive advantage, Smith spent years developing the Qualtrics software platform, focusing on ease of use and customization to meet the unique needs of each customer. He also invested in research and development to stay ahead of the competition and ensure that his platform remained the best in the market. This allowed Qualtrics to establish itself as a leader in the customer experience management industry and attract a wide range of customers, from small businesses to large enterprises.

Qualtrics' success was further solidified when the company was acquired by SAP in 2018 for $8 billion. The acquisition was a testament to the strength of the company's competitive advantage and the unique value it brought to the market.

In conclusion, Ryan Smith's ability to leverage his unique expertise in survey research and his focus on developing a user-friendly, customizable software platform allowed him to build a sustainable competitive advantage for Qualtrics. This, in turn, allowed the company to establish itself as a leader in the customer experience management industry and attract a wide range of customers.

Forming the Right Team

Creating and leading a team with the right set of skills and experience is crucial for the success of any entrepreneurial venture. As an entrepreneur, you may have the vision, the idea, and the drive to succeed, but it is the team that will help you achieve your goals.

One of the most important reasons to create and lead a team with the right set of skills and experience is to have the necessary knowledge and expertise to tackle the challenges that arise during the venture. A diverse team with a variety of skills and experiences can bring fresh ideas, different perspectives, and the ability to solve problems creatively. This is especially important when dealing with complex problems that require expertise in multiple areas.

Another important reason to create and lead a team with the right set of skills and experience is to ensure that the team can execute the plan effectively. A team with the right skills can help ensure that the plan is executed efficiently and with a high degree of quality. This can lead to increased customer satisfaction, increased revenues, and increased profits.

In addition, a well-chosen team can help mitigate risk for the entrepreneur. Startups are inherently risky, and a strong team can help minimize that risk by providing guidance and support in areas such as finance, marketing, and operations.

Finally, a strong team can help to attract investors and customers. Investors are more likely to invest in a venture that has a strong team with a track record of success. Similarly, customers are more likely to buy products and services from a company with a team of experts who can provide high-quality service and support.

In summary, creating and leading a team with the right set of skills and experience is critical for the success of any entrepreneurial venture. A strong team can bring diverse skills, execute plans effectively, mitigate risk, and attract investors and customers. As an entrepreneur, it is important to focus on building a team that can achieve the goals of the venture.

WAYS TO IDENTIFY AND RECRUIT THE RIGHT TEAM MEMBERS

Recruiting the right team members is essential for the success of any startup. It is important to identify individuals who have the necessary skills and experience to carry out the tasks required to meet the objectives of the startup. Below are some techniques for identifying and recruiting the right team members:

- **Define the Roles and Responsibilities:** Before recruiting team members, it is important to define the roles and responsibilities of each team member. This will help in identifying the required skills and experience for each role.
- **Identify the Required Skills and Experience:** Once the roles and responsibilities are defined, it is important to identify the required skills and experience for each role. This can be done by analyzing the tasks required to meet the objectives of the startup.

- **Look for Individuals with a Track Record of Success:** Look for individuals who have a track record of success in their previous roles. This can be done by reviewing their work history and accomplishments.

- **Leverage Your Network:** Leverage your personal and professional network to identify potential candidates for the roles. Garnering referrals from trusted sources can be a great way to find individuals who have the necessary skills and experience.

- **Use Online Resources:** Use online resources such as LinkedIn and other professional networks to identify potential candidates for the roles. These resources can provide information on a candidate's professional history, skills, and endorsements.

- **Conduct Interviews:** Conduct interviews with potential candidates to assess their skills, experience, and fit with the team. It is important to ask questions that are relevant to the role and responsibilities.

- **Check References:** Check references to verify the skills and experience of potential candidates. This can provide valuable insight into their work history and accomplishments.

By following these techniques, entrepreneurs can identify and recruit the right team members who have the necessary skills, experience, and fit to help the startup achieve its objectives.

TECHNIQUES FOR MANAGING AND MOTIVATING A TEAM

Managing and motivating a team is a critical component of entrepreneurial success. It is important to have a cohesive and motivated team to ensure that your startup is successful in the long run. Here are some techniques for managing and motivating a team:

- **Communication:** You need to ensure that everyone is aware of the goals and objectives of the company and their individual roles in achieving those objectives. Regular meetings, updates, and feedback are all essential to keep everyone aligned and motivated.

- **Empowerment:** Give your team members autonomy and responsibility for their work. This will make them feel more invested in the success of the company and will give them a sense of ownership over their work. It will also enable them to make decisions and take actions that will drive the company forward.

- **Recognition and Rewards:** Recognize the hard work and achievements of your team members. Celebrate milestones, accomplishments, and successes. Also, offer incentives and rewards to encourage and motivate them to perform at their best.

- **Continuous Learning and Development:** Encourage your team members to learn new skills and expand their knowledge. This will not only benefit them personally, but also add value to your company. You can offer training opportunities, mentorship, and other resources to help them develop their skills.

- **Trust:** Trust is essential to building a strong and motivated team. You need to trust your team members to do their job, make good decisions, and act in the best interests of the company. This will help build a culture of mutual respect and accountability.

- **Culture**: Create a positive and engaging work culture that fosters collaboration, creativity, and innovation. This will help keep your team members motivated, engaged, and invested in the success of the company.

In summary, managing and motivating a team is critical to the success of any startup. By using these techniques, you can build a strong and cohesive team that is committed to achieving the goals and objectives of the company.

How Kavita Shukla Formed the Right Team

Kavita Shukla, the founder of The FRESHGLOW Company, has built a successful team to support her mission to create sustainable solutions for the world's challenges. Shukla's background is in microbiology, and she wanted to tackle the issue of food waste, which is a significant problem worldwide. Shukla's solution was FreshPaper, a natural, biodegradable paper that keeps fruits and vegetables fresh longer.

Shukla started working on FreshPaper while she was still in college. When Shukla graduated, she began selling FreshPaper at farmer's markets and local stores, but it was not until she won a social innovation competition that she was able to start her company officially.

With funding from the competition, Shukla founded The FRESHGLOW Company and began building her team. Shukla believed that the right team was critical to the success of The FRESHGLOW Company, and she made sure to hire people with diverse backgrounds and experiences. Shukla hired people who were passionate about sustainability and reducing food waste, and she made sure they shared her values and vision for the company.

To maintain the company's vision, Shukla created a collaborative and open work environment that encouraged innovation and creativity. Shukla also prioritized the development of her team and provided opportunities for them to learn new skills and grow within the company.

The FRESHGLOW Company's success is a testament to the importance of building the right team. The company has expanded its product line and distribution, and FreshPaper is now sold in over 35,000 stores worldwide. Shukla's focus on building a team that shared her values and vision helped her create a sustainable business that is making a positive impact on the world.

Is the Opportunity Real?

Identifying real entrepreneurial opportunities is crucial for entrepreneurs; it can determine the success or failure of a business. It is important for entrepreneurs to understand the problem and craft a competitive solution that meets the needs of customers and outperforms competition. This process involves identifying and evaluating problems, researching, and gathering data to define the problem, generating and evaluating ideas, screening and refining solutions, and leveraging unique advantages to create a sustainable competitive advantage.

One of the key elements of opportunity identification is defining the problem. Entrepreneurs need to identify a problem they can solve that is important to customers. Understanding the problem and its impact on customers is essential for creating a competitive solution that meets their needs.

Crafting a competitive solution involves generating and evaluating ideas and examining competing products. Entrepreneurs need to screen and refine solutions to ensure that they are viable and can outperform competition. Creating a sustainable competitive advantage is important for long-term success, and this involves leveraging unique advantages and building a team with the right set of skills and experience.

Building the right team is another key element of opportunity identification. Entrepreneurs need to identify and recruit team members with the right skills and experience and manage and motivate them to achieve the goals of the business.

Summary

Identifying real entrepreneurial opportunities is a critical aspect of starting and growing a successful business. Entrepreneurs must be able to recognize problems they can solve and develop a competitive solution, build a sustainable advantage, and assemble a team with the right set of skills and experience. The process of identifying opportunities involves thorough research and analysis, as well as creative thinking and a willingness to take risks. By following the techniques and methods outlined in this chapter, entrepreneurs can increase their chances of finding and capitalizing on real opportunities that can lead to long-term success. Ultimately, the ability to identify and pursue real entrepreneurial opportunities can make the difference between a successful and a failed venture.

17. Next Steps

Let the future tell the truth,

and evaluate each one according to his work and accomplishments.

The present is theirs;

the future, for which I have really worked, is mine.

Nikola Tesla

Prolific Inventor and Father of the Modern Electronics Industry

With this journey now complete, you are ready to use the Opportunity Analysis Canvas to identify and analyze entrepreneurial ideas.

The Opportunity Analysis Canvas

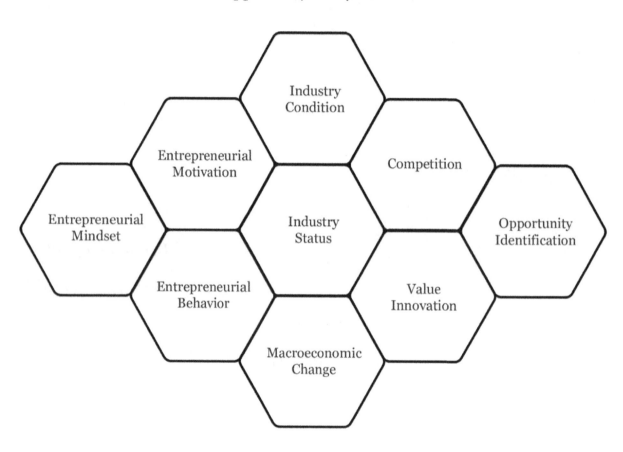

By studying this book, your awareness of entrepreneurial mindset, motivation, and behavior has expanded. You appreciate the roles of markets and industries in entrepreneurial opportunities. You understand value innovation and the fundamentals of opportunity identification as key elements of entrepreneurial action.

DEVELOPING YOUR OPPORTUNITY ANALYSIS CANVAS

As you develop your Opportunity Analysis Canvas, reflect on your work from prior questions in this book, and update your responses to align with this checklist:

1. Based on your prior thoughts on Thinking Entrepreneurially, summarize your level of need for achievement, individualism, control, focus, and optimism.
2. Based on your prior thoughts on Seeing Entrepreneurially, summarize your level of self-efficacy, cognitive motivation, and tolerance for ambiguity.
3. Based on your prior thoughts on Acting Entrepreneurially, summarize your confidence, risk tolerance, interpersonal relationship skills, and social capital.
4. What are the knowledge and demand conditions for a new business idea that you may develop?
    a. Include at least three references that support the demand conditions.
5. For this business idea, what is the life cycle stage of your industry, and the existing industry structure?
    a. Include at least three references that support the lifecycle stage and industry structure.
6. For this business idea, what are the demographic, psychographic, technical, and societal changes as well as the political and regulatory forces in your industry?
    a. Include at least three references that support these changes and forces.

7. For this business idea, what factors can your team eliminate, reduce, raise, and create?

    a. Describe why the factors that you selected for the value curve are important to customers.

    b. Include at least three references that support the factors that you've selected.

8. For this new business idea, discuss how the learning curve influences your success, the complementary assets that are critical to develop for your venture, and the reputation of your competitors.

    a. Include at least three references that support your analysis.

9. For this new business idea, summarize why the problem is real, how your team's solution creates value for stakeholders, the types of advantage that you all possess, and your ability to build the right team.

    a. Include at least three references that support your analysis.

DEVELOPING THE BUSINESS MODEL

Developing your business model is the next step in your entrepreneurial journey.

As a precursor to writing the business plan, the business model describes the logic of how an organization creates, delivers, and captures value sustainably.

While the term *business model* is very popular today, the concept dates to the earliest days of business, and simply defines how an organization will make money.

A comprehensive model defines how the products or services of a business serve customer needs, at what price, through what manufacturing and distribution channels, and at what financial benefits and costs to the business.

With a well-developed business model, you can test your assumptions and strategy with prospective customers. They may affirm parts of the business model and reject others. This early customer discovery and validation is valuable to adapting the business model, and perhaps the fundamental product or service idea itself, before authoring a full business plan.

WRITING THE BUSINESS PLAN

This experience of hearing your customers' needs and wants in reaction to the business model allows you to write a well-researched business plan. With a customer-validated business plan, you can raise financial capital (if needed) and proceed with launching the venture.

Now, get to work!

Best wishes in fulfilling your entrepreneurial goals.

Made in the USA
Middletown, DE
24 August 2024

59669196R00190